D1138583

Ian Kershaw

The Greatest Play in the History of the World . . .

methuen | drama
LONDON • NEW YORK • OXFORD • NEW DELHI • SYDNEY

METHUEN DRAMA
Bloomsbury Publishing Plc
50 Bedford Square. London WC1B 3DP. UK
1385 Broadway, New York, NY 10018, USA

BLOOMSBURY, METHUEN DRAMA and the Methuen Drama logo
are trade marks of Bloomsbury Publishing Plc

First published in Great Britain 2018
Reprinted 2019

Copyright © Ian Kershaw, 2018

Ian Kershaw has asserted his right under the Copyright, Designs
and Patents Act, 1988, to be identified as author of this work.

Cover design: Grant Archer
Cover image © Elspeth Moore

All rights reserved. No part of this publication may be reproduced
or transmitted in any form or by any means, electronic or mechanical,
including photocopying, recording, or any information storage or retrieval system,
without prior permission in writing from the publishers.

Bloomsbury Publishing Plc does not have any control over, or responsibility for,
any third-party websites referred to or in this book. All internet addresses
given in this book were correct at the time of going to press.
The author and publisher regret any inconvenience caused if addresses
have changed or sites have ceased to exist, but can accept no responsibility
or any such changes.

No rights in incidental music or songs contained in the work are
hereby granted and performance rights for any performance/presentation
whatsoever must be obtained from the respective copyright owners.

All rights whatsoever in this play are strictly reserved and application
for performance etc. should be made before rehearsals by professionals and
by amateurs to The Agency (London) Limited, 24 Pottery Lane, Holland Park,
London W11 4LZ. No performance may be given unless a licence
has been obtained.

A catalogue record for this book is available from the British Library.

A catalog record for this book is available from the Library of Congress.

ISBN: PB: 978-1-350-08964-8
ePDF: 978-1-350-08965-5
ePub: 978-1-350-08966-2

Series: Modern Plays

Typeset by Country Setting, Kingdown, Kent CT14 8ES
Printed and bound in Great Britain

To find out more about our authors and books visit www.bloomsbury.com
and sign up for our newsletters

THE GREATEST PLAY
IN THE HISTORY
OF THE WORLD . . .

Ian Kershaw

Actor **Julie Hesmondhalgh**

Director	**Raz Shaw**
Designer	**Naomi Kuyck-Cohen**
Lighting Designer	**Jack Knowles**
Sound Designer	**Mark Melville**
Producer	**Tara Finney**
Stage Manager	**Philip Hussey**
PR	**SM Publicity**
Graphic Design	**Grant Archer**

This production would not have been possible
without the support of Arts Council England
and the team at the Royal Exchange Theatre, Manchester.

Julie Hesmondhalgh | Actor

Julie is a BAFTA-nominated actor. She trained at LAMDA and is best known for her award-winning portrayal of Hayley Cropper in *Coronation Street*, a role she left after 16 years and won multiple awards for including an RTS Award for Best Performance (2013), a National TV Award for Best Serial Drama Performance (2014) and a Best Actress Award at the British Soap Awards (2014).

Theatre credits include: *The Almighty Sometimes*, *The Greatest Play in the History of the World . . .* , *Wit* (Manchester Theatre Award 2017/ nominated for a TMA), *Black Roses: The Killing of Sophie Lancaster* (Manchester Theatre Award 2013), *Blindsided* (all Royal Exchange Theatre); *The Report* with Lemn Sissay, *God Bless the Child* (Royal Court).

Television credits include: *Catastrophe*, *Doctor Who*, *Broadchurch* (BAFTA nomination for Best Supporting Actress 2018), *Happy Valley*, *Black Roses* (RTS Award for Best Actress 2015), *Moving On*, *Inside No. 9*, *Banana*, *Cucumber*, *The Dwelling Place*, *Pat and Margaret*, *The Bill*, *Dalziel and Pascoe*.

Radio credits include: *What Maisie Knew* (BBC Radio 4), *Dead Weight*, BBC Festival of Poetry, *Anansi Boys*, *I Told My Mum I Was Going on an RE Trip*, *Glue*, *Over Here, Over There*, *The Fix*, *Fat Little Thing*, *Zola: Blood* (Drink), *Cleaning Up*, *Queens of the Coal Age*, *Deadheading*, *Dead Clever*, *Dead Pan*, *Glue*, *Pick of the Week* (Radio 4), *Exile*, *The Verb*, *Torchbearers* (BBC Radio 3).

Film credits include: *Pond Life* with Bill Buckhurst, *Peterloo* directed by Mike Leigh.

Julie has recently been awarded an Honorary MA in Performing Arts from the University of Chichester and the Freedom of the Borough of Hyndburn. She is a speaker for Arts Emergency and founder of Take Back, an award-winning political theatre collective in Manchester.

Ian Kershaw | Writer

Theatre credits include: *The Greatest Play in the History of the World . . .* (Traverse Theatre/Royal Exchange Theatre); *Bread and Roses, Union Street, Star-cross'd* (Manchester Theatre Award, all Oldham Coliseum); *The Mist in the Mirror* (national tour); *Cinderella* (Duke's Lancaster); *Get Ken Barlow* (Watford Palace Theatre); *Candyland* (Bruntwood Award, Royal Exchange Theatre); and short plays for JB Shorts, The Miniaturists and Take Back Theatre. For Monkeywood Theatre Company: *The Manchester Project* (HOME); *We're Not Really Here* (The Lowry).

Television credits include: *Coronation Street, Cold Feet* (ITV); *Medici: Masters of Florence* (Netflix); *EastEnders, Castles in the Sky* (film); *Death in Paradise, The Dumping Ground, Holby City, Doctors, Casualty* (BBC); *The Mill, Shameless* (Channel4).

Radio credits include: *Lost and Found* (Radio Academy Award), *Porcelain* (*The Trial for the Killing of Sophie Lancaster*), *Closely Observed Trains, Autobiography of a Nobody, Alan and Jean's Incredible Journey, Raft to Bondi*. He also created and wrote two series of 6x30' comedy *Pick-Ups* and a 4x30' comedy *Cleaning Up*.

Raz Shaw | Director

Theatre credits include: *The Greatest Play in the History of the World . . .* , *Wit* (UK Theatre Award for Best Director), *Things of Dry Hours* (also The Gate Theatre), *The Trestle at Pope Lick Creek* (also Southwark Playhouse) (all Royal Exchange Theatre); *The God of Soho, A Midsummer Night's Dream, Romeo and Juliet* (Shakespeare's Globe); *Wie es Will Gefällt* (Bremer Shakespeare Company); *The Talented Mr Ripley* (Northampton Theatre Royal); *Tommy* (Prince Edward Theatre); *Gambling* (Soho Theatre); *Othello, Woman In Mind, Be My Baby* (Salisbury Playhouse); *Jenny Fawcett* (Soho Theatre/Pleasance); *Edgar and Annabel* (AracaWorks Festival NYC); *Torn, Factory Girls* (Arcola); *A State of Innocence/Photos of Religion* (Theatre503); *Belly* (Old Red Lion).

He is currently developing *Joybubbles*, a new musical by Carl Grose and Alex Silverman. His first book *Death and The Elephant: How Cancer Saved My Life* was published in March 2018.

Naomi Kuyck-Cohen | Designer

Theatre credits include: *Trap Street* (New Diorama); *And Yet It Moves* (Young Vic); *Nightclubbing* (The Lowry and UK tour); *Passin' Thru* (Lyric Hammersmith); *Dreamplay* (The Vaults); *Trigger Warning* (Tate Modern); *In My Dreams I Dream I'm Dreaming* (Theatre Royal Plymouth); *I, Myself and Me* (Curve Theatre and UK tour); *Rise: Macro vs. Micro* (Old Vic New Voices); *FEAST* (Battersea Arts Centre).

Jack Knowles | Lighting Designer

Jack trained at the Central School of Speech and Drama.

Theatre credits include: *The Importance of Being Earnest* (Vaudeville Theatre); *Machinal, They Drink it in the Congo, Boy, Carmen Disruption, Game* (Almeida); *Happy Days, Parliament Square, Our Town, Twelfth Night, A Streetcar Named Desire, Wit, The Skriker, There Has Possibly Been an Incident* (Royal Exchange Theatre); *Dan and Phil: Interactive Introverts, The Amazing Tour is Not on Fire* (world tours); *Instructions for Correct Assembly, 2071* (Royal Court); *Caroline, or Change* (Chichester Festival Theatre/Hampstead Theatre); *Circle Mirror Transformation* (HOME); *Wonderland* (Nottingham Playhouse); *Beginning* (National Theatre/Ambassadors Theatre); *Barber Shop Chronicles* (National Theatre/West Yorkshire Playhouse/Australian tour); *Committee* (Donmar Warehouse); *4.48 Psychosis, Reisende auf einem Bein, Happy Days* (Schauspielhaus, Hamburg); *Junkyard, Pygmalion* (Headlong); *The Forbidden Zone* (Salzburg Festival/Schaubühne, Berlin/Barbican); *Cleansed* (National Theatre); *A Sorrow Beyond Dreams* (Vienna Burgtheater); *Lungs, Yellow Wallpaper* (Schaubühne, Berlin); *Night Train* (Schauspiel, Köln/Avignon Festival/Theatertreffen).

Mark Melville | Sound Designer

Mark is an award-winning composer and sound designer for theatre, dance and film. He trained at Leeds College of Music.

Theatre credits include: *Where Do We Stand?* (Northern Stage); *1984* (Emilia Romagna Teatro, Italy); *Frankenstein* (Royal Exchange Theatre); *Flight* (Vox Motus/Edinburgh International Festival/The McKittrick, New York); *Rules for Living* (English Touring Theatre/Royal and Derngate); *Charlie Sonata, Midsummer Night's Dream* (Edinburgh Royal Lyceum); *Human Animals, Violence and Son, God Bless the Child* (Royal Court); *Yer Granny, The Beautiful Cosmos of Ivor Cutler, My Shrinking Life, Knives in Hens, Miracle Man, Empty* (National Theatre of Scotland); *Tomorrow* (Vanishing Point/Cena Contemporânea Festival/Brighton Festival/Tramway).

Mark is also a frequent collaborator with director Louie Ingham.

Tara Finney | Producer

Tara qualified as a corporate solicitor before starting her theatrical career as Resident Assistant Producer at Theatre503. She then worked as Producer for Iris Theatre and as Associate Producer at Company of Angels, before going freelance. She runs Tara Finney Productions, and also production company Tiny Fires Ltd with director Paul Robinson; their inaugural production, *My Mother Said I Never Should* starring Maureen Lipman and Katie Brayben, received critical acclaim during its run at St James Theatre in spring 2016 – www.tinyfires.co.uk. Tara is currently also Interim Producer and Programmer at the Stephen Joseph Theatre, Scarborough.

Theatre credits include: *Joking Apart, Build a Rocket* (also Edinburgh Fringe and Latitude), *The 39 Steps* (Stephen Joseph Theatre); *A Brief History of Women* (59E59, New York); *World Factory* (Young Vic, New Wolsey Theatre); *Helver's Night, Theatre Cafe York* (York Theatre Royal); *Alice Through the Looking Glass, Richard III, Alice in Wonderland, Julius Caesar* (St Paul's Church); *Desolate Heaven, Where the Mangrove Grows, ELEGY, Life for Beginners* (Theatre503).

Philip Hussey | Stage Manager

Philip is based in Manchester and has worked in stage management for twenty years.

Theatre credits include: *Cosmic Scallies, Persuasion, A Streetcar Named Desire, The Skriker* (Royal Exchange Theatre); *Whisky Galore* (Oldham Coliseum); *The Changing Room, Wizard of Oz* (Sheffield Crucible); *Ghosts* (HOME); *The Bear* (Pins and Needles Productions).

Other work includes: projects with Hull Truck Theatre, RASA, National Theatre, Lip Service, English Touring Theatre, West Yorkshire Playhouse, Arts Theatre London, Phoenix Dance Theatre and Esplanade Singapore, as well as around thirty productions at Manchester's Royal Exchange Theatre. His next project is as DSM on Jean Genet's *The Maids* at HOME, Manchester.

Tara Finney Productions (TFP) is a multi-award nominated, independent theatre production company. TFP was founded to produce *Land of Our Fathers* which was Time Out's 2013 Fringe Show of the Year. In March 2015, she produced *WINK* starring *Harry Potter and the Cursed Child* star Sam Clemmett. This January, TFP's 20th anniversary production of Enda Walsh's *Disco Pigs* starring Evanna Lynch transferred to the Irish Repertory Theatre, New York, garnering a Critics' Pick from the *New York Times* and extending for two weeks. TFP also has a number of exciting shows in development.

Theatre credits include: *The Greatest Play in the History of the World . . .* (Traverse Theatre/Royal Exchange Theatre); *Disco Pigs* (Irish Repertory Theatre, New York/Trafalgar Studios); *Burkas and Bacon Butties* (VAULT Festival); *Ishq* (Sadler's Wells, as associate for Serendip Productions); *All Our Children* (Jermyn Street Theatre); *good dog* (national tour, for tiata fahodzi and Watford Palace Theatre); *MUTED* (Bunker Theatre, for Interval Productions); *The Acedian Pirates* (Theatre503); *And Then Come the Nightjars* (national tour, as associate for Theatre503 and Bristol Old Vic); *Land of Our Fathers* (Found111/National Tour/Trafalgar Studios/Theatre503); *WINK* (Theatre503).

TFP's productions have been nominated for over twenty-five awards including Off West End Awards, UK Theatre Awards, the Susan Smith Blackburn Award and the Chita Rivera Awards, New York.

tarafinney.com

@tara_finney

facebook.com/tarafinneyproduction

instagram.com/tarafinneyproductions

Manchester's **Royal Exchange Theatre Company** transforms the way people see theatre, each other and the world around them. It was named Regional Theatre of the Year in 2016 and School of the Year at The Stage Awards 2018. The Spring–Summer Season features work from an incredible array of artists from across Manchester and beyond. It includes a new adaptation of Chekhov's *The Cherry Orchard* translated by Rory Mullarkey, Sarah Frankcom directing Maxine Peake in Samuel Beckett's master-piece *Happy Days* and a new play by Associate Artist Maxine Peake, *Queens of the Coal Age*, opening in June. Associate Artists RashDash and new partners Yellow Earth bring their distinctive performance styles to The Studio.

royalexchange.co.uk

@rxtheatre

facebook.com/rxtheatre

instagram.com/rxtheatre

The Greatest Play
in the History
of the World . . .

For
JAM

Author's Note

Julie Hesmondhalgh is my favourite actor in the world. She also happens to be my wife. She asked me to write her a play. I did. This is it.

It's about love.

Raz Shaw is my favourite director in the world. He is not my wife. He tells my wife where she should stand and sometimes, like in our marriage, she agrees with him.

The play is about life and living and what happens when we've gone.

It's also about other things too.

I once saw an elderly man looking at a swing-bin in a hardware shop; it looked like he'd never bought a swing-bin in his life, someone else had always bought the swing-bin but that someone else wasn't here any more. He had to buy the swing-bin. The play is kind of about that.

And shoes.

It's also about shoes.

When I was a teenager my friend took his own life and I saw his shoes in the place where he'd kicked them off for the last time. I paired them up and placed them near to a wall. I thought I was tidying things up. This I now feel was a gross invasion of privacy. I should have left that for his mum to do. They were her son's shoes.

It's also about space and the stuff that's up there. The International Space Station is the size of a football pitch, weighs 450 tons and flies over our heads fifteen times a day, it never fails to amaze me. There is no mention of that in the play.

The Golden Record is even more amazing. Copies are attached to *Voyager One* and *Two*. They are records made out of gold (obvs). *Voyager* was launched in 1977 and will continue through space long after we've gone. There is definitely mention of that in the play.

In short – it's a play about life and lost love and found love.

It has heart, lots of heart.

And shoes.

The play as it is here would not be anything like it is without Julie Hesmondhalgh's ruthless editing, beautiful suggestions and love and support.

The first production would be nothing without Raz Shaw's brilliant mind. The stage directions listed here evolved through his and Julie's hard work, determination and their mutual resentment.

A Note on Production

The play is to be performed by one actor.

There are a number of characters referred to in the play, these characters can be realised for the audience by 'placing' character-appropriate footwear which can be previously set in shoeboxes or (as encouraged by Julie Hesmondhalgh) generously donated by unsuspecting audience members.

A bare stage, save for a number of shoeboxes.

Music tracks from NASA's 'Voyager Golden Record' play.

Morse code and ship horns from the Golden Record play as the lights fade.

One

Actor *(pre-recorded)*   *Voyager* is NASA's scientific program employing two robotic probes – *Voyager One* and *Voyager Two*. In 1977 these two probes were launched into space to study the outer Solar System. Each *Voyager*, travelling at over 35,000 miles per hour, carries with it a twelve-inch golden phonograph record. The 'Golden Record' contains sounds and images portraying the diversity of life and culture on Earth. Its intention: to communicate to extra-terrestrials the story of our world.

Lights up to reveal **Actor** *has arrived.*

Two

Actor *walks us down Preston Road.*

Actor   Preston Road is a busy road.

A busy motorway junction down there.

A busy hospital up there.

There's a bad bakers there that sell good pies.

And a Polish shop here that sells knock-off tobacco.

There's a pub that never opens here.

An off-licence that never closes there.

These two things are probably linked . . . ?

Most – things – are . . .

There are rows and rows of houses all the way along, some private, some rented, all of them dirty because of the traffic.

As is customary, odd numbered houses are on one side. Here.

Even numbered houses on the opposite side. Here.

She smiles, happy they've created the road, and places the shoebox down – Number 28.

The time is four-forty a.m.

She opens the shoebox and pulls out a pair of tatty carpet slippers –

At 28 Preston Road, a thirty-one-year-old man named Tom –

She places the slippers on top of the box – **'Tom'.**

Actor   – wrestled with a too-high-tog duvet, not too high for the time of year – mid-December – but too high due to the fault on his boiler that meant it would cough into life and pump out as much heat as it chose whenever it chose to.

Tom lay star-fished in his pants and ironic band T-shirt, victim to the boiler and its random decision to suddenly squirt its hot water through the guts and intestines of the house to rise, fart and gurgle through the paint-stuck radiators. Blinking awake, he turned his head from the Artexed ceiling, peering past the dust-topped glass of water, to see the bedside clock displaying the time – zero four-four-zero.

Tom was immediately aware of the palindromic numerical neatness at play, he was a fan of all things symmetrical. Although generally he preferred words to numbers, thinking of himself as more of a 'words man' than a 'numbers kind of guy' – which may be of interest if you're the sort of person who likes to categorise people into two distinct groups – 'numbers' and 'words' – a person very much like Tom.

Tom believed that for every ying there was yang – he knew a vegetarian could fall in love with a meat-eater and a cat person could marry a dog person; therefore, Tom felt, that being a words kinda guy he would, one day, meet and fall in love with a numbers kinda girl. If only he could find a numbers kinda girl. Over his thirty-one years, twenty of which he'd been curious about the opposite sex, he'd searched for a numbers woman to fit his word-man self. But his search had proved, hitherto, fruitless.

In preparation for his eventual meeting with a numbers girl, he had tried to find common ground. For example, he had grappled with the mathematical structure of iambic pentameter –

She beats out iambic pentameters.

the | struc | ture | of | pent | a | meter –

all metre in fact –

from | the | great | po | ets
to | the | sim | ple | yet com | plex
struc | ture | of | hai | ku.

Although he delighted in the inherent maths of poetry Tom was ultimately far more concerned with words. He liked words. He loved words. Particular current favourites being *cherish*, *marzipan* and *traffic-cone*. Words that, to be honest, Tom felt had been sadly lacking in the canon of some of the great sonneteers.

His love of symmetry ensured he noted it whenever and wherever it cropped up – from a beautifully balanced mini-roundabout to the perfect golden arches of the McDonald's 'restaurant' logo, a place Tom despised not for perhaps the many obvious reasons but because of one particular event that took place there that we'll touch on presently.

Tom's birth date had symmetry to it and he secretly hoped that when he died it would be on a symmetrical date so that his gravestone would look symmetrically pleasing. It didn't occur to him that he wouldn't actually be there to witness these perfectly symmetrical dates etched into a marble headstone or more probably a plastic plaque fixed to a wooden bench overlooking his favourite view at the top of the steps in Whitby. Still these were some of the thoughts that regularly occupied him. But his principal preoccupation, the one recurring musing, the constant cogitation that was less of a thought and more of a fear was this: Tom was terrified that he was treading water, that he was stuck, in short – that his life had stopped. He forced his eyes shut and tried to go back to sleep.

What felt like an hour passed before Tom blinked open one eye to check the time again and saw that it was now . . . four-forty a.m. The clock was relatively new – he'd ordered it online from Argos six weeks ago, it had been delivered safe and sound and when he'd plugged it in it had worked perfectly well. He'd even taken the precaution of buying a clock with a back-up battery feature that would ensure the clock would continue to work during a power failure. Not that Tom should have been unduly worried about missing his alarm, he didn't have anything to get up for, full-stop. *But* by choosing an alarm clock with a battery back-up function it suggested that there would be *something* he would get up for *someday*. He had not given up. Tom had hope.

He sat up, stared at the clock and waited and . . . nothing happened. *Zero four four zero.*

The world seemed still. He listened. There were no sounds: no wind, no sirens, no traffic on the usually very busy road, nothing, just . . . nothing. He turned on the bedside lamp, waited a few moments for the eco bulb to yawn and stretch into life before he swivelled out of bed, stamped into his slippers and padded to the window.

Slicing open the curtains he peered out.

Darkness enveloped the road: there were no streetlamps, no car headlights, and the multitudinous Christmas lights that usually twinkled in and all over the houses on Preston Road were lifeless. There was no light, no movement, nobody and nothing, just nothing . . .

Nothing that is until he saw, across the road, in an almost mirror image of his house – a lighted bedroom with the curtains sliced open where –

She opens another box and places another pair of carpet slippers down opposite **Tom** *as the* '**The Twenty Six-Year-Old Woman in Over-sized Bowie T-Shirt'.**

Actor   – a twenty-six-year-old woman in comfortable pants and oversized David Bowie T-shirt, stood looking at him, looking at her. He caught his breath, stepped back and let the curtains fall back into place. He didn't want to be seen as some kind of Peeping Tom. Particularly as his name was Tom and if word had got out it would have been all too easy for the –

She picks up two shoeboxes –

– unruly kids at Number 58 –

She empties the boxes of mismatched well-worn trainers out: '**The Unruly Kids at 58'.**

Actor   – to make his life more of a misery than it already was. Tom wasn't a voyeur or even nosy – he preferred the term 'interested' – Tom was interested in what was going on, on Preston Road. He thought of himself as a community minded person, even though he never actually left the house to do anything in the community, partially subsumed as he was by apathy or ennui or a feeling that could now be neatly summed up as 'meh'. Apart from the fact that he never left the house, Tom would have been an ideal member of the local Neighbourhood Watch group, although he had politely declined the invitation to the founding meeting organised by the elderly couple next-door at Number 30, whilst reluctantly agreeing to join the Facebook group.

She opens another box with two pairs of slippers.

Tom had nothing against the elderly couple at Number 30, Mr and Mrs Forshaw. Yes, he had been slightly put out by the constant building noises that had emanated from their backyard for months on end; the endless sawing, drilling, welding, and the hum, thrum and sparking of electricity. But Tom had been far more concerned with the fact that he didn't know what the Forshaws were actually building in their very large and, from Tom's perspective, very annoyingly placed shed. He had however noted that all the noises had suddenly ceased on September the second, a date that Tom couldn't have known fell shortly after Mrs Forshaw's consultant had given her the news that there was nothing more that could be done.

Having placed the slippers down, she points out '**Mr & Mrs Forshaw**'.

Actor   Eighty-one-year-old Mr Forshaw had long fostered the belief that seventy-six-year-old Mrs Forshaw was slightly hard of hearing, a belief that was entirely without foundation. What Mrs Forshaw had was selective deafness: if Mr Forshaw made a stupid comment or said something idiotic she simply *chose* not to hear him.

The two of them had, until recently, spent their days happily crosswording, making soup and pottering around their large garden shed building the thing they called 'The Kakudmi'.

She holds Mrs Forshaw's slippers.

Mrs Forshaw had for many years been a science teacher at a long underfunded comprehensive school, and had dedicated her career to developing exciting ways to reach into the minds of the bored teenage pupils, forced by the latest government educational guidelines to study a general science subject.

She taught basic chemistry by showing them how to make their own whisky distilleries, physics by teaching them how to build time machines and biology – well she didn't think she necessarily had to worry about that component as they all seemed to have a head start on her there.

She puts the slippers down.

There was one particular lesson that always inspired Mrs Forshaw's pupils, a lesson so legendary it was talked about in the corridors and locker rooms for *minutes* afterwards. The lesson would always begin with one primed and fused pupil daring to ask about the tattoo on Mrs Forshaw's forearm. In that moment she would smile, knowing that it was time, and, lifting her cardigan sleeve to reveal the tattoo, she would read the inked words aloud –

'*Per aspera ad astra*'.

Mrs Forshaw would then take off her spectacles, gather her breath and introduce her class to the 'Golden Record'.

Light change.

Three

Actor (*pre-recorded*)   A committee was assembled to decide which images and sounds should go on to the Golden Record and this committee was chaired by Carl Sagan. You would have liked Carl Sagan. He was a real personality, a dope smoker, a rock-star scientist who ruminated on a great many things in our world and beyond. Amongst many of the things Sagan did was to serve as Professor of Astronomy at Cornell University; there he wrote over a dozen books and became known as 'the gatekeeper of scientific credibility'. He had so many careers all colliding and overlapping, it was as though he knew he wouldn't live to an old age – he wanted to cram it all in. This, via Carl Sagan, is my advice to you all – cram it in.

Light change. She moves to Preston Road – picks up Mr Forshaw's slippers.

Four

Actor   Mr Forshaw was a poet. He'd written a great deal of poetry over the last seven years and although he hadn't made a single penny from his writing, it had, nonetheless helped to give him some purpose post-breakdown. He had also been a teacher – a lecturer of literature at university level, no less, and had been on a steady career path until his 'interruption'. Like with many mental health issues, there hadn't been any one specific trigger for his collapse, although Mrs Forshaw had always secretly suspected that his meticulous study of the Romantic poets might have had something to do with it. In particular Mr Forshaw's obsessional pursuit of the notion that the word *love* would have been better communicated if the poets had used a symbol rather than the actual word 'love', which Mr Forshaw believed had lost its power and weight due to overuse.

Mr Forshaw had conducted his final lecture entirely with semaphore flags and a Casio calculator looped to an amp and an overhead projector. He'd very quickly found himself pensioned off on medical grounds and had subsequently thrown himself into writing his own sonnets mainly in squiggle and symbol form before eventually finding his way back into the world of words via Facebook, ornithology and a night-school course in metalwork.

So Mr and Mrs Forshaw were a nice couple, engaged in community matters and who had been the driving force in setting up the Preston Road Neighbourhood Watch Group after a spate of vandalism targeting several cars that most people suspected was the handiwork of 'the unruly kids at Number 58'.

Tom, next door, hadn't witnessed any of 'the unruly kids at Number 58' causing mayhem and, to be fair, if anyone would have noticed, it would have been Tom, thanks to his keen 'interest' in the comings and goings on Preston Road and the unique absence of nets and blinds in his lounge window. Tom could often be spotted polishing the windowsill whenever there was some burst of activity on the road. And he would, as a matter of course, take to cleaning the window itself, inside only, whenever someone new was moving in somewhere nearby. The last time being when the twenty-six-year-old woman in the oversized Bowie T-shirt had moved in to the rental house opposite – Number 27.

Inside Number 27, the twenty-six-year-old woman in the comfortable pants and oversized Bowie T-shirt, surprised by Tom peering at her, had herself taken a step back from the window allowing the curtains to fall back into place.

She didn't know Tom, and aside from the day of the Great Bin Escape and a time she'd seen him take in a small parcel from an Argos delivery guy, he always seemed to be in his front room. Polishing his windowsill. When she left for work in a morning he was polishing the windowsill. When she returned home in the evening he was there, polishing the windowsill. It appeared to her that the man never actually left his house – or moreover, his windowsill.

'The Great Bin Escape' was the morning after 'the big storm'.

The weather girl on the local news with the gap in her front teeth and unfeasibly straight hair had said that a *hurricane* was due but the twenty-six-year-old woman in the oversized Bowie T-shirt didn't agree with the gap-toothed straight-haired weather girl that a genuine hurricane was indeed approaching. She had once lived in a country where there were *real* hurricanes; she had lived there with a man who had smashed her heart to bits and had, in a small act of revenge, returned to England in his favourite David Bowie T-shirt.

It was a *storm* that had blown her wheely-bin right down to the Polish shop, not a hurricane – a *storm*.

The morning after the storm the man from Number 28, who rarely moved from his windowsill, had surprised the woman from Number 27 by actually leaving his front room. He was out to recapture his own bin at the same time as she was out hunting for hers and this chance encounter was the only time they had ever spoken. He'd made what may or may not have been a joke about the bins that, as far as she could tell, had referenced the film *The Shawshank Redemption*. She couldn't be sure because, as he'd called to her, a screaming ambulance had cut through the middle of them.

Although she'd not really heard his quip, she'd laughed all the same, not uproariously just a tentative 'haaa'. Noting his reaction, she had felt a pang of worry that she hadn't perhaps displayed the requisite amount of jollity and had added an uncertain 'ha yeah'.

They had stared at each other for a moment before he said something else that she also missed, something that she was pretty sure contained the word *hurricane,* and that had really pissed her off. She had quickly and quietly dismissed him as an idiot before abruptly jabbing her hip into her bin to tilt it back and drag it home.

Unbeknownst to her, then as now, she and Tom had shared something in common – she too was terrified that she was being left behind, that she was stuck in a rut; in short – that her life had stopped.

Light change.

Five

Actor (*pre-recorded*)   Carl Sagan and his committee assembled one hundred and sixteen images including instructions on how to play the disc from simple drawings based in mathematics and science, which they believed would be understood by aliens.

Other images show details of human anatomy and reproduction along with cultural aspects of life on earth – people eating, drinking and dancing.

People having a good time.

People cramming it all in.

Light change. **Actor** *is back to Preston Road.*

Six

Actor   Over at Number 28, Tom knew that sleep was now out of the question and that he had to do something.

Downstairs in the front room he clicked on his computer, and as it Brian-Eno-sing-songed into life, he checked the time (four-forty a.m.) and started to write. He didn't know exactly *what* he was writing other than it was some sort of play and that at the end of the night he would have finished it and that it would be the greatest play in the history of the world. He decided there and then that he would call his play *The Greatest Play in the History of the World*.

The play would be about a woman, a woman he decided to call Sarah – he'd always fancied Sarahs. He hadn't known much about relationships aged eleven but he'd known he'd wanted Sarah, the first Sarah, Sarah the First, Sarah who loved to play football on the estate he grew up on.

He'd wanted her to hold his hand, he'd wanted her to kick her ball to him, or even at him. He'd wanted her to notice him but she never did.

She moves through the audience and volunteers a pair of Uni-Sarah shoes from an audience member.

The second Sarah, he'd met at uni.

She shows us **Uni-Sarah***'s shoes.*

Actor   Sarah 2 was a fellow student and she was gorgeous, the most beautiful woman Tom had ever seen but Tom instinctively knew that she was out of his league.

She hands Uni-Sarah's shoes back to the audience member (advising her that she'll be back for them).

The next Sarah in his life . . .

She scans the audience to find a pair of Sarah-like shoes, volunteers them and shows us Sarah –

– was the most *significant* Sarah; he referred to her as '*Sarah the Significant*'.

*She places '***Sarah the Significant***' next to Tom.*

Actor   They'd had an intense relationship, full of passion, desire and what Mr Forshaw, next door, would have described as *&%. We'll come back to Sarah in a bit.

She hands Sarah back to her owner – again saying that she'll be back.

She focuses in on Tom . . .

In the living room at Number 28 Tom decided, as he sat bathed in the light of his computer screen, that his heroine would therefore be called Sarah. He typed the name S-A-R-A-H, and then fast forwarding fearfully to the highly probable scenario wherein the Pulitzer Prize Committee would trace the real-life Sarahs in his past, he let inspiration strike, leant forward and promptly deleted the H.

He nodded, delighting in his own cunning. The heroine of *The Greatest Play in the History of the World* would be called *Sara*.

She moves to 'The Twenty-Six-Year-Old Woman in Oversized Bowie T-Shirt' aka 'Sara'.

Over at Number 27, the twenty-six-year-old woman in the oversized Bowie T-shirt, whose name you may be interested to know was Sara, had rolled herself a cigarette, opened the curtains a smidge and was now focused on Tom busy at his computer in his downstairs front room. Dismissing the fleeting thought that he could be looking at porn as he didn't have nets or blinds at his window, she wondered what exactly he could be doing at four-forty in the morning. It was a brief thought as altogether bigger things were currently occupying Sara's mind – thoughts like why, other than at Tom's house and Mr and Mrs Forshaw's house across the road, there were no signs of life or movement on Preston Road? And, more pressingly, why had time apparently stopped?

Light change.

Seven

Actor (*pre-recorded*)   The Golden Record contains scientific images and photographs of people, animals and insects. The committee, led by Carl Sagan, chose not to include images of war, poverty, disease, crime, ideology or religion.

There are spoken greetings in fifty-five different languages, the line in English – *'Hello from the children of planet Earth'* – was recorded by Carl Sagan's six-year-old son. There's also music on the disc – from Peruvian Panpipes and Pygmy Girls from Zaire to Bach, Beethoven, Mozart and Chuck Berry. The Beatles had gladly given permission for 'Here Comes the Sun' to be used, only for it to be blocked by their record company.

Eight

Actor *returns to Preston Road.*

Actor   Before looking out of the curtains again, Sara had turned her alarm clock off and on and off and on and off and on and yet the time had stayed the same. She knew she could easily take the clock to pieces, feeling confident in her technical ability to examine the simple circuit board for abnormalities, but before she did that she had to rule out the obvious. She decided to check the time elsewhere: she turned on her phone that lay charging on the floor, the cord not quite stretching to her bedside table, and the phone always off as she'd been woken up too many times recently by multiple email alerts from the local Neighbourhood Watch Facebook Group outlining the latest whereabouts of the unruly kids at Number 58. The phone, when it had finally Appled into life had displayed the time as *zero four four zero*. Sara stared at it for a long time, pulling the Bowie T-shirt over her knees to keep warm and ruing the fact that the broken boiler the landlord had said would be fixed before Christmas had remained unfixed.

Sara was famed for her intolerance of cold and once when a young, trendy-bearded PE teacher had made the mistake of publicly joking in the staff room that her constant chilliness may have had something to do with her vegetarianism, she'd called him a dick and this exchange had, she delightedly discovered later, abruptly ended his stealthy and slightly unnerving pursuit of her – a pursuit that had begun shortly after she'd started working there at the beginning of term.

Sara held her phone in one hand, counting elephants out loud until, reaching eighty-two elephants, she'd accepted that time had indeed simply stopped. Sara was attempting to take in the enormity of this fact when an email alert from the Neighbourhood Watch Facebook group had interrupted her train of thought. But this wasn't the usual group message, no, this message had been sent to just two members – Sara, and Tom at Number 28. And moreover the message consisted of just one word. This one-word had sent Sara scurrying back to the bedroom window.

Light change.

Nine

Actor (*pre-recorded*)   The disc also contains, recorded in Morse code, the message – *'Per aspera ad astra'*. Along with recordings of the natural symphony and cacophony of the world – volcanoes, earthquakes and thunder etc., there are also soundtracks of engines and ship horns, footsteps and heartbeats, and the simplest, most human expression of all – a kiss.

She blows a kiss.

Light change. She returns to Preston Road.

Ten

Actor   Tom was in the middle of an intricately crafted sentence on the physical appearance of the heroine in his play when it dawned on him that the character of Sara he'd constructed was completely informed by –

She retrieves Sarah (shoes) from the audience.

– his old love Sarah.

She places the shoes down – Sarah.

Although he tried to limit his Facebook stalking of Sarah to just one or two peeks a day, this was going to be one of the days when he exceeded his planned rationing. He typed in her name, opened her page and Sarah's lovely face grinned out at him from her profile picture. Well not at *him* of course, but at the man who had no doubt taken the photograph:

She volunteers a pair of Marcus-style shoes from a member of the audience and holds them up for us to see – '**Marcus**'.

Actor   Tom's best friend – Marcus.

Or should I say, Tom's *former* best friend – Marcus.

She drops Marcus's shoes to the floor, in front of the volunteer and tells him she'll come back to him.

She picks up Sarah and moves her to Tom.

Sarah and Tom had met at a pub during their respective works' Christmas parties; they had both independently slipped outside on the pretence of having a cigarette, even though neither of them smoked. After the obligatory soulless scroll through their smart-phones and the casual nod and hiya reserved for strangers outside pubs they'd drifted into conversation. Sarah had complimented Tom on his carpet slippers and Tom had made a nice comment appertaining to Sarah's shoes.

Sarah was interested to know why Tom was shod in carpet slippers outside a pub, in early December, in the rain. For some time Tom's footwear of choice had been a pair of tatty desert boots, the only comfortable fit for his weird and oddly sized trotters. The slippers, he explained, had been a 'joke' Christmas present from his colleagues who had attempted to cajole him into trying them on, before pinning him down, stripping him of his old faithfuls and ramming his toes into the fur-lined tartan. Feeling anxious from the forced public humiliation Tom had gone outside on the pretence of having a cigarette, and it was here he'd met the other Sarah, the all-consuming Sarah, Sarah-soon-to-be-Significant, the Sarah of these shoes.

Sarah told him that she was outside because the people in her party had started playing games, not quite pass-the-parcel but more of a 'truth or dare' type game that had started to get a little mean as the wine fizzed and the lager flowed. When the game had turned to 'which famous people we most resemble' Sarah had felt that a fight was on the horizon – there was *always* a fight when that game was played, usually when someone was jokily likened to Arnold Schwarzenegger – no woman ever liked that.

Tom laughed and introduced himself and they shook hands, and in the brief moment he'd felt her hand in his, when she'd said that her name was Sarah, Tom heard the tinkling of a hundred bells in his head and felt an immediate fizzing in his chest. He knew right then, with one-hundred-per-cent certainty that he would marry her, that they would have children and they would live happily ever after.

He was wrong.

Light change.

Eleven

Actor (*pre-recorded*)   In the early 1990s, as *Voyager One* headed towards the outer reaches of the solar system, Carl Sagan was among those who managed to persuade NASA to turn the spacecraft's camera back towards Earth, which was by then billions of miles away.

An image was taken and beamed back to Earth, where it was initially dismissed as a worthless nothing – a blank sheet of black with a soft blurred streak of late summer's day haze, peppered with specks of dust.

One late night, one scientist, alone with the image, zoomed in and saw, amongst the dust, a tiny blue-Bic'd dot on an lower case i.

Earth.

On that pinhead was everything that breathed, pulsed and died. Everything that ever existed, everything that ever was and everything that ever will be. Every moment in time, every grain of sand, every drop of water, every heart that beat, every eye that saw, every hand that ever touched – all there in a minute insignificant speck of blue floating on a needle shaft of sunlight in the pitch of night.

Light change. **Actor** *is back on Preston Road.*

Twelve

Actor   Tom clicked on another photograph on Sarah's Facebook page, a page that didn't have privacy settings – a detail that, Tom had decided, would be sufficient to ensure a downgrading of the charge of stalking to one of 'merely interested'.

The next photograph to pop up on screen was a selfie of Sarah and Marcus aka The Utter Shit.

She parks Sarah to address Marcus.

The Utter Shit had been Tom's best friend, they'd grown up on the same estate, attended the same school and had even kept in touch when they'd both left to go to separate universities.

They'd visited each other at their respective campuses, Tom awkward amongst Marcus's new friends, Marcus totally at ease with Tom's fellow students. Marcus was always at ease with anyone and everyone was at ease with him. Even Uni-Sarah who Tom had instinctively known was out of his league had readily stumbled into the night with Marcus, another of his conquests, another notch on his heavily scored bedpost.

Tom, on the other hand, had never been much of a Lothario. Aside from losing his virginity to Marcus's older sister, Angela, who preferred to be called Spider and who now resided in an open prison with a Panadol addiction, he'd only had a few drunken fumbles with equally drunk and fumbly students at uni.

All of this changed the night he met Sarah the Significant outside the pub whilst wearing carpet slippers. They'd laughed, they'd connected and within the hour had ditched their respective works parties to get a taxi back to Preston Road, stopping off at the off-licence to pick up an overpriced what-the-heck bottle of champagne en route.

That night, everything had suddenly made sense to Tom: every piece of music, poetry and art and every star in the night sky, every beat of a butterfly's wing and every note of a bird's song all collided in a riot of lust and passion. Tom felt that this was the moment everything in his life had been leading up to.

They'd stayed up all night, drinking and holding hands, looking at the stars, reading poetry – Sarah was also a lover of words. They'd traced the scars of exes past and Tom secretly thought that this was it, there would be no other – not after this night and day and next night and next day when they suddenly realised that they should probably have something to eat. Tom fried eggs and spinach while Sarah, sexy like in films, in Tom's ironic band T-shirt, looked on from her perch on the kitchen unit. The food was left to go cold as they tumbled into bed again and again and again. Reality dawned the next morning when they both had to leave for work, but they had met up at lunchtime and throwing caution to the wind, had made love in Sarah's knackered old Toyota on the tenth floor of a city centre multi-story car park. And it was there in the steamed up car, as the latest world-changing guitar-driven indie-landfill crackled on the radio, that Tom had told Sarah that he loved her.

Tom always traced events back to this moment and wondered if he'd been too rash, too hurried, too much. And he often speculated that had he played his hand differently, perhaps subsequent events would have played out differently too.

Tom knew that if he hadn't gone to the pub and hadn't been forced to wear slippers, therefore feeling humiliated and anxious, then he wouldn't have slipped outside and met – (*Showing shoes.*) Sarah the Significant.

Tom also knew that if they hadn't gone back to Preston Road and if he hadn't professed his love for her in the car park a few days later then he wouldn't have ever introduced her to his then best friend, Marcus. And Marcus wouldn't have been round at Preston Road a few weeks later to see Sarah reach for his coat as he was leaving and notice her top ride slightly up, showing a glimpse of the lace trim of her knickers peeking out of the top of her jeans.

And Marcus wouldn't then have sent Sarah a friend request on Facebook before 'accidentally' bumping into her in town the night she'd gone to celebrate her friend's birthday, without Tom. And Marcus wouldn't have told Sarah that he hadn't accidentally bumped into her at all, he knew exactly where she was going to be, he'd seen it on Facebook.

And Marcus wouldn't then have struggled to breathe and his mouth wouldn't have dried up and his pupils wouldn't have dilated as Sarah wouldn't have told him that she too had wanted him from the very first moment they had met, that she felt it had been truly inevitable that they would get together: after all – their star signs were totally compatible.

Light change.

Thirteen

Actor (*pre-recorded*)   Right now, *Voyager One* is over twelve billion miles away from Earth, journeying through Interstellar Space beyond the planets in our solar system. Its electrical instruments are expected to last another few years until its internal generators cease to supply power. It will then continue to drift in no particular direction, heading through the darkness, the depths, the unknown, the unfathomable loneliness of eternity.

Unless –

Unless someone, or something, picks it up.

Light change. **Actor** *is back to Preston Road.*

Fourteen

Actor   The affair had gone on unnoticed by Tom for months and months and months; even though the truth of it was staring him in the face he hadn't seen it, unconsciously he had turned his back on it.

It was a genuine shock to him when Marcus and Sarah sat him down in a local branch of McDonald's – thinking no doubt that a public place would be best to minimise fuss and violence – and told him they had fallen in love, that they couldn't help it, that after all she was a Pisces and he was a Scorpio.

Tom hated star signs.

He had continued stirring his styrofoamed 'coffee' long after Sarah and Marcus had left. He didn't taste the coffee, he knew it would be bitter and undrinkable no matter how many sachets of sugar he poured in. He tried to absorb the end of the chapter, the turning of the page, the burning of the book, as all around him people cheerlessly devoured their Happy Meals.

It had only really, truly, honestly sunk in for Tom after Sarah had left Number 28 Preston Road with all her things – all her things except for one.

He'd managed to get to Tesco's, he'd managed to negotiate the aisles of people holding hands, sharing shopping lists and rowing over trolleys. He'd managed to walk most of the way home, until the pumping of the blood in his ears – like the noise of the hot water working its way through the guts and intestines of his house – had become unbearable.

The pulsing pressure worked its way through his arteries and rose, farted and gurgled into his heart which now threatened to leap out of his chest, determined to escape either through his chest wall or up out of his throat, out of his mouth and out on to the pavement outside number 58 Preston Road. Tom looked to the pool of vomit, the shopping bags still cutting into his hands, as the unruly kids looked on.

The unruliest kid, the thirteen-going-on-thirty-year-old with the skinhead, earring and home-drawn tattoos, had looked to him and said, 'Are you alright, mate?' and 'Do you want some water or summat?'

Tom had tried to thank him but couldn't, he couldn't speak until he finally managed to somehow get through his front door at Number 28, placing his shopping bags on the floor to see the one thing that Sarah had forgotten to take, the one thing that reminded him of the night they met, the one thing that was actually, in a grammatical and, in a symmetrical sense, two things – a pair . . .

She examines Sarah's shoes.

That was the moment in the day of the week of the month of the year when he finally took in the deceit, the end of days, the loss – and in and amidst that loss Tom found his voice and wailed and wailed and wailed. He had wailed so loudly that Mrs Forshaw had woken from her medicine-induced slumber in her front room bed at Number 30 and had known in that moment that it would all end alright for the nice man next door – she just knew it.

Tom didn't know it. His future, as far as he could see, was like the 'Golden Record' on *Voyager One* – a treasure-trove of memories, of images, music, laughter, song, all drifting through space – unheard, unnoticed, unloved.

And all these months later, here, at four-forty in the morning, Tom stared at the Facebook-uploaded picture of Sarah and Marcus, and scrolled down, knowing that he'd see the thing that he'd seen a hundred times before. The thing that was like a knife between his shoulder blades, slowly freezing his muscles as it worked its way through into his heart. And sure enough there it was again – there was Sarah's hand, a glint of a diamond on a ring on a finger on a hand on a bump on a stomach – none of which had anything to do with Tom.

Tom stared.

Tom drifted.

Tom was in deep space.

The soft ping of an email alert drew Tom back to Earth – it was a message from the Neighbourhood Watch Facebook Group, a message that hadn't gone to the whole group but only to him and one other member. He clicked on the message and saw that it consisted of just one word . . . and that word was '*HELP!*'.

Next door, at Number 30, on a bed in the downstairs front room, Mr and Mrs Forshaw were lost in deep sleep. Mrs Forshaw was dreaming, like many people in the winter of their years, of the past – the good times.

It was her wedding – she and Mr Forshaw were in a farmer's field under a tatty marquee, held together with string and Sellotape to keep out the rain. Her charity-shop wedding dress and his cheap suit were both edged with mud as they danced on the grass – their first dance, to their song, The Beatles' 'Here Comes the Sun'. She rested her head on his shoulder and breathed in his scent, an aftershave with woody-pine top notes. Breathed him in and revelled in the feel of his hand on her hip. She was happy, deliriously happy. But then the scent of pine was suddenly overpowering, she saw pine needles moving across the grass towards her, like ants heading for a nest, the needles piled on top of each other building and growing into a tower that stretched then turned into a wave that crashed over her, knocking her to the ground.

Mrs Forshaw blinked open her eyes to find a little bit of sick on her nightie. Mr Forshaw, next to her, slept soundly, oblivious to his wife's discomfort.

She lay still, waiting to catch her breath, she smelt pine and remembered how earlier that day they'd had their yearly debate over which Christmas tree to get, if indeed they should bother. They had assessed the pros and cons of real versus artificial and dead versus pot before Mr Forshaw had placed a telephone order to the local garden centre from whence a dead pine was duly despatched.

And now Mrs Forshaw lay awake looking at the tree as the lights twinkled away, a rave for the fairy she had made as a child – some old lace trim for a dress and glittery pipe-cleaner wings surrounding a clothes-peg body with its felt-tipped joyful face. She shared a smile with the angel before the spreading pain in her chest kicked to the marrow of her bones, making her wince. Winded, holding herself for a moment and not wanting to make a noise that would disturb her sleeping husband, Mrs Forshaw made a decision. She reached to the travel alarm clock and pressed down the alarm button – glancing at the display – *zero four four zero*.

She traced the tattoo on her forearm –

'Per aspera ad astra' –

And feeling the pain ease, she snaked her toes into her slippers and Mrs Forshaw rose from her deathbed.

Padding softly across the Axminster, carefully removing the various tubes and wires as she moved, she took a last little look at Mr Forshaw sleeping soundly before she slipped out of the room and headed to the kitchen at the rear of the house.

Light change.

Fifteen

Actor (*pre-recorded*)   Everything that has ever been and everything that ever will be, will continue to expand like a vibration, a sound, an echo through time and space. Like a stone dropped into the centre of a pond creating ripples that continue long after the stone rests on the mud-filled bottom. Everything will vibrate and ripple long after we, the earth and everything that ever will be, simply ceases to be.

She joins in, speaking over the pre-recorded.

All of our yesterdays, our todays and tomorrows reaching out to the very edges of the universe before the threads of time pull and strain, contract, and everything will begin to repeat but in reverse. Everything that has ever been and ever will be will happen again.

All our days, our lives again in an instant – like the flick of a switch, like the click of fingers – (*Clicks fingers.*) like a kiss – (*Blows a kiss.*) speeding through time until everything that has ever been and everything that ever will be – collapses in on itself.

Light change. **Actor** *moves back to Preston Road.*

Sixteen

Actor   The fluorescent tube blinked into life as Mrs Forshaw filled the kettle. The kitchen was cold, it was always cold, even in the height of summer, the sun never reaching the rear of the house thanks partly to geography but also because of the excessively large shed that occupied the stone-flagged yard.

Mrs Forshaw bobbed the kettle on before lifting her nightdress off and over her head, and stood for a moment, naked except for a pair of new pants that barely clung to her disappearing hips. She looked at her ghostly figure reflected in the kitchen window and saw the faint criss-cross ley-lines of illness where faded scars met more recent angry cuts. She thought of the pain that had gnawed at her bones for the longest time and that was now absent.

Pulling on a freshly laundered nightdress hanging over the radiator, she squeaked open a cupboard and eased out a shoebox.

She shows us an old shoebox.

The lid, long sealed, and unopened for years, initially refused to yield but Mrs Forshaw managed to prise it open allowing the air and light to rush in, revealing its treasures.

She places the shoebox centre (but doesn't open it).

She reached in for the soft-pack of cigarettes and book of matches. In a long practised but forgotten motion she tapped out a fag, placed it between her lips and struck the match. The tobacco, powder-keg dry, easily sparked and the rush of leather –

of butter –

of stale caramel –

flooded her mouth, throat and what was left of her lungs.

She allowed the smoke to gently fall from her nose and a sense of total and complete happiness filled her and surrounded her. She saw in her reflection in the window that she was glowing – a golden, radioactive Ready-Brek light.

To a passerby, if there could possibly have been such a thing, this could have looked like death, but it was far from that. Mrs Forshaw was alive, truly alive and very at peace; she knew she was one of only three people awake on the Earth right now and that felt good. The kettle reached boiling point, clicked off and Mrs Forshaw, her thoughts full of Tom and Sara, made herself her last cup of tea.

Meanwhile at 28 Preston Road, Tom had absorbed the message, and, realising that he would have to leave his house for the first time since the Great Bin Escape Day, had a quick spray of some old aftershave in an attempt to mask the scent of night-time temperamental boiler-induced sweat. The aftershave was so old that it smelled of nothing other than pine-cones but at four-forty in the morning it was the best he could do. And so Tom, feeling as ready to face the world as ever (i.e. not at all) and opting to keep his slippers on, kitten-pawed it to Number 30, ringing the bell again and again.

Deciding against waiting too long, he headed up the side alley to gain access to Mr and Mrs Forshaw's back yard.

Across Preston Road at Number 27, Sara had stubbed out her rolly, pulled on a pair of jeans and had headed out of the front door, momentarily distracted by her phone still glowing and showing the time – *zero-four-four-zero*.

She felt the slight slip and snap of an iced-over pothole under foot and realised that in her haste she hadn't changed into sensible shoes. Deciding that she should plough on regardless, she carefully hopped, skipped and slippered across the deserted Preston Road, ringing the bell at Number 30, and pulling the oversized Bowie T-shirt tight around her as though it was a blanket.

At exactly four-forty Mrs Forshaw looked to the remaining contents of the shoebox – comprising wholly of a bundle of papers tied with a frayed red ribbon addressed to Tom and Sara. She replaced the lid, had a good hacky cough, opened her laptop, typed 'HELP!' and clicked '*Send*' from the Neighbourhood Watch Facebook Group before heading out of the kitchen door.

She managed to navigate the few stone flags from the house to the huge shed, and unlocking then squeaking open the door, she stepped inside, flicked on the light and turned to face 'The Kakudmi'.

It was time.

Meanwhile, in the front room of Number 30, Mr Forshaw was lost in a dream. In it he was sitting on a bench overlooking the sea, with the peal of a church bell behind him. The bell's ring was insistent, not celebratory, something not right, and as he looked away from the sea he snored himself awake and realised that the church bell was actually the chime of the doorbell. Mr Forshaw quickly turned to check on Mrs Forshaw and seeing she wasn't there and panicking that she'd gone to answer the door in her frail state, Mr Forshaw leapt out of bed like an octogenarian ninja and creaked and groaned to the front door.

Outside Number 30, anxious Sara, anxious finger on doorbell, was growing ever anxious – she was sure she'd seen somebody duck down the side alley as she approached and wondered if this somebody was the reason the Forshaws had sent out a call for help via the unusual channel of the Neighbourhood Watch Facebook page in the early hours. Either way, Sara was certain that she wouldn't be investigating any time soon, she'd seen enough Scandi-dramas to know that, huge woolly-jumper and 'back-up-on-the-way' notwithstanding, you simply do not navigate dark alleyways alone at four-forty a.m.

A figure eventually loomed into view through the obscured deep Flemish glass and the door swung open to reveal Mr Forshaw. Sara blurted out that she'd received a message – what was going on?

Mr Forshaw stared blearily at Sara – what indeed was going on?

And then deep inside his head a neuron farted a miniscule electrical signal through a synapse into another neuron – in short, the penny dropped – Mr Forshaw's eyes focused with the realisation of a seismic revelation: It was time!

At the back of the house, Tom had somehow managed to stay upright as he excitedly traversed the slippy-stone-flagged alleyway towards the pulsing noise and glowing light emanating from the Forshaws' large shed. For many years Tom had puzzled over what they were actually building in there, but until now he hadn't caught the merest glimpse.

But now as he stood at the threshold of the shed, he drank in the sight of the thing that the Forshaws had spent the last seven years building together, the thing that had helped Mr Forshaw deal with his enforced retirement and the thing that had helped Mrs Forshaw deal with her diagnosis by enabling them to plan their future, their present and their past . . . The Kakudmi.

As his eyes adjusted to the ultra-sun-on-snow bright light, Tom caught his breath and stared and stared and stared.

In the perennially cold kitchen of Number 30 Mr Forshaw grabbed the shoebox containing the red-ribbon tied bundle of papers that he and Mrs Forshaw had written many, many moons ago, and thrust the box into Sara's hands, telling her that all the answers were there.

Meanwhile Tom inside the shed, gaze fixed on Mrs Forshaw bedecked in slippers, nightie, leather flying-hat and goggles, saw her step into what Tom would later describe as a freestanding shower cubicle – possibly from B&Q's 'Piccadilly' range with acrylic base, aluminium profile and clear safety glass.

Mr Forshaw appeared, closely followed by Sara clutching the shoebox, bellowing to Mrs Forshaw that he was here, everyone was here! Mrs Forshaw laughed, clapped and shouted to Mr Forshaw, calling him by his first name: Tom.

Eighty-one-year-old Tom Forshaw grabbed a matching leather flying-hat and goggles, and shouted to Mrs Forshaw that he was on his way, calling her by her first name: Sara.

The twenty-six-year-old Sara in the oversized Bowie T-shirt stared at the seventy-six-year-old Sara in the flying-hat and goggles and everything made sense.

The thirty-one-year-old Tom in the ironic band T-shirt stared at the eighty-one-year-old Tom in the flying-hat and goggles . . . and nothing made sense.

Both pairs of the same person separated by fifty years were occupying the same space in different times.

Mrs Forshaw told Mr Forshaw that at exactly four-forty she'd been shaken awake by the disease. It was penetrating her bones, moving into the fibre, the very marrow of her and she knew that she had to act – this may not work but at least this way they had a glinting speck of a glimmer of a chance. They had hope.

Mr Forshaw adjusted his goggles, Mrs Forshaw blew a kiss to her younger self, took Mr Forshaw's hand in hers and closed the door.

A series of buttons and switches were pressed, there was a
growing whirring noise and a gust of wind so strong that Tom
the younger remarked to Sara the younger that it felt like
a hurricane. She, of course, chose to ignore this ridiculous
comment and this further confirmed Tom's suspicion that she
was slightly hard of hearing.

There was a blinding end-of-the-world atomic-bomb-like
flash of light, followed by a strangely disappointing pop, then
darkness.

Lights out.

Seventeen

Lights up.

Actor   Sara correctly surmised that Mr and Mrs Forshaw,
like the Golden Record years before them, were now
journeying into the far reaches of space and time.

Tom, in his tatty tartan slippers and Girls Aloud T-shirt,
looking more of an idiot than anyone would think possible,
noted that the time was now four-forty-one.

They had crossed Preston Road to Sara's place for a shot of
whisky, marvelling at the steady pulse of street lights, the
twinkling of Christmas LEDs, and the roar and flash of the
blues and twos of a passing ambulance.

Normality.

The world moving again.

They had then collided with two of the unruly kids from
Number 58 who noticing Tom and Sara's inappropriate
footwear had asked

'Y'alright?'

Tom and Sara despite having witnessed the most extraordinary
four-forty in time immemorial, mumbled in a very British

way that they were fine. The lads told them they were keeping an eye on things, after a recent spate of burglaries, saying:

'This road's good, a good place to live, we want it to stay like that.'

As they'd moved away, Tom and Sara had agreed that people shouldn't be so judgemental about the unruly kids at Number 58, vowing to copy them into the Neighbourhood Watch Facebook Group at the earliest opportunity.

She places all the shoes from the unruly kids at Number 58 back in the box.

Sara poured Tom a large shot of her particularly strong and fiery burny-burny home-made whisky that the man in a faraway place had taught her to make before smashing her heart to bits.

She thought of the man in the faraway place and realised that, at this very moment, right here, right now, she had made her peace, with him, with life; she'd moved on.

She toasted the air, revealing as she did, the tattooed words on her forearm −

'Per aspera ad astra'.

Tom, spotting the inked words, and without hesitation grabbing the chance to finally impress, chinked his glass against hers, and beaming, toasted:

'Through hardship to the stars!'

It worked. Sara, impressed by Tom's immediate and correct translation, thought for the first time that perhaps he wasn't quite as much of an idiot as he'd first seemed. As time passed and the whisky and conversation flowed Sara began to glow with the growing realisation that Tom was a words man, perhaps the words man she'd always been looking for: she herself being, after all, a numbers kind of girl.

And when Tom remarked on the amazing coincidences of the night − how Sara and Sara had the same tattoo and wasn't it funny how they all shared the same names, Sara realised there was much work to be done, but that she had a lifetime to explain everything to him. Not now though, not tonight. First Tom had to go home and finish writing his play, the play that he would no longer call *The Greatest Play in the History of the World* out of fear of mean-hearted critics with their easy two-word reviews – 'It isn't' – settling for the slightly downscaled *The Greatest Play in the History of the World . . . of Number 28 Preston Road.*

Tom struggled with heartburn that had nothing to do with the home-made whisky and everything to do with the complete and utter acceptance that he was never meant to have been with a Sarah after all, it was always meant to be a *Sara* – and not any Sara but this Sara, this specific Sara right-here-and-right-now Sara.

He knew that they would trace the scars of exes-past and that he would fall in love, and he would say it to her far too soon and that it wouldn't matter because it would be true and she would say it back and they would live happily ever after.

And for once . . . Tom was right.

It had been fated, not written in the stars but beyond them. Long before they were even born it had been decided that they would meet right here and right now and that they'd go on to marry in a knackered marquee in a muddy farmer's field – a field where Sara would lean into Tom and smell his piney aftershave while they first-danced to 'Here Comes the Sun'.

And that they'd honeymoon in Whitby where they'd climb up the steps to the Abbey, to find a bench, a bench overlooking the sea, a bench on which they one day planned to affix a plaque, but on reaching it would find a plaque already in place.

A plaque that simply said '*&%'.

She opens the shoebox – it glows with light.

After Tom had returned to Number 28, Sara opened the shoebox that Mr Forshaw had given her and pulled out . . .

He pulls out a bundle of papers tied up with red ribbon, unties the ribbon and leafs through the pages –

The pages contain images, one hundred and sixteen images all told, including instructions on how to build a Kakudmi with words and simple drawings based in mathematics and science.

And on the final page of the bundle is a question.

A question to Sara.

A question from Sara.

A question that Sara immediately knows is the lesson.

A question that will inevitably be prompted by the raised hand of one primed and fused pupil daring to ask about the tattoo on her forearm.

She smiles and rolls up **Sara**'s *sleeve to reveal the tattoo on her arm – 'Per aspera ad astra'. She reads the question:*

If you had been on Carl Sagan's committee, what one thing would you have fought to have had put on the *Golden Record*: a message, a sound, an image, a thought, a feeling?

It's up to you.

Each and every one of you has to think what it is that you would want on your very own Golden Record. The proof of your life, your existence, your very being as it's pushed out into the inky depths of nothingness for all eternity.

A record of you that will live on long, long, long after you've gone.

What is it that you would want to be preserved for eternity?

A photograph of the tip of Everest? An Indian spice market? Or the view from a bar overlooking the ocean in Big Sur, California?

The taste of a tear, of blood, of sweat. The sound of the rustle of a daffodil as it blooms. The smell of coarse salt and sharp vinegar on seaside fish and chips. That moment when

someone notices you for being you and gets it – they get you –
that feeling, that! The touch and grab and snap of clenched
skin, muscle and flesh in that moment of complete and utter
hunger-sating ecstasy.

The unexpected creak of the door when the person you
wanted to see more than anything in the world walks in to
surprise you.

The bubbles up your nose when your best friend makes you
laugh when you're both drinking lemonade through straws.

Summer sun on a long wintered face; a bonfire, a firework,
a plastic windmill on your pram.

The sound of a bee, a bird, a poet. That song, that piece of
music, that yell of your crowd as your team score that goal.

The wet-warmth of snowman-building-mittens drying on a
radiator.

A cup of tea! Just the way you like it.

Two pairs of slippers warming in front of a gas fire.

She folds the paper and tucks it away.

Or would it be the feel of your mother's hand walking you to
your first day at school, or the hand held in yours of the first
person you fell in love with or the last hand-hold of the
person you've loved most in your whole life – the last hand
hold of that person who loved you right back.

And how could you cram in all that experience, all that
memory, all that heartache and love into one tiny track on
a twelve-inch golden phonograph record drifting through
space and time waiting to be found and felt by something,
someone . . .

With a word or a symbol?

She mimes the symbol.

Or perhaps with that simplest most uniquely human
expression of all . . .

She blows a kiss.

Sound of a breath as the lights pulse like stars before snapping out.

When the lights come up the **Actor** *has gone, leaving just two pairs of slippers onstage . . .*

The End.

*&%

D1138590

Navigating Panic Attacks

WELBECK
BALANCE

NEWHAM LIBRARIES

90800101146882

ABOUT THE AUTHOR

Rita Santos is a clinical psychologist who specializes in cognitive behavioural therapy (CBT), anxiety and anxiety disorders. She completed her clinical training (1998) and specialized in CBT for anxiety disorders (2000) in Lisbon, Portugal. In order to pursue her interests further, Rita completed a PhD on cognitive aspects of anxiety and performance in London (2007), conducting cutting-edge psychology research including functional Magnetic Resonance Imaging (fMRI) of the brain. Her research provided the main empirical underpinning of a novel theory of anxiety: attentional control theory.

Following a period as a post-doctoral researcher and lecturer at Royal Holloway, University of London, she also pursued further specialist CBT training in the UK for anxiety-related difficulties (2011). During her career she has developed a broad range of skills, including extensive academic experience (conducting research, publishing papers and delivering undergraduate- and postgraduate-level teaching), and wide clinical expertise (working privately, in psychiatric hospitals, in student support centres, and in the NHS). She currently provides CBT training and supervision, and works as a cognitive behavioural psychotherapist.

OTHER BOOKS IN THIS SERIES

Navigating Loneliness
Navigating Sleeplessness
Navigating Stress

Navigating Panic Attacks

Understand Your Fear and
Reclaim Your Life

Dr Rita Santos PhD

WELBECK
BALANCE

A Trigger Book

Published by Welbeck Balance

An imprint of Welbeck Publishing Group

20 Mortimer Street

London W1T 3JW

First published by Welbeck Balance in 2021

Copyright © Rita Santos, 2021

Rita Santos has asserted her right under the Copyright, Designs and Patents Act, 1988, to be identified as the Author of this work.

All rights reserved. No part of this publication may be reproduced, stored in a retrieval system, or transmitted in any form or by any means, electronically, mechanical, photocopying, recording or otherwise, without the prior permission of the copyright owners and the publishers.

A CIP catalogue record for this book is available from the British Library

ISBN

Trade Paperback – 9781789562552

Typeset by Lapiz Digital Services

Printed in Great Britain by CPI Group (UK) Ltd, Croydon CR0 4YY

10 9 8 7 6 5 4 3 2 1

Note/Disclaimer

Welbeck Balance encourages diversity and different viewpoints. However, all views, thoughts, and opinions expressed in this book are the author's own and are not necessarily representative of Welbeck Publishing Group as an organization. All material in this book is set out in good faith for general guidance; no liability can be accepted for loss or expense incurred in following the information given. In particular, this book is not intended to replace expert medical or psychiatric advice. It is intended for informational purposes only and for your own personal use and guidance. It is not intended to diagnose, treat or act as a substitute for professional medical advice. Professional advice should be sought if desired before embarking on any health-related programme.

www.welbeckpublishing.com

To Alice Baptista, Maria and Antonio Silva, my late grandparents who could not read or write, and worked so hard all their lives to make sure I could.

CONTENTS

INTRODUCTION

If you bought this book, you are either curious about panic attacks, experience them yourself, or know someone who does. You may have heard about what it is like to have a panic attack and want to find out more, or you know all too well how it feels to have one – how frightening and distressing it is – and would like to understand them better.

All of us have been and will go through anxious situations at various points in our lives. For example, taking exams, going to the dentist, having injections, speaking or performing in public, having to stand up for yourself or others, getting a piercing, or asking a manager for a raise, among many, many others. Experiencing nervousness and anxiety in these situations is entirely normal and, for better or worse, we have on the whole managed to cope with such situations.

Panic attacks feel somewhat different.

Let's face it, "panic" is a frightening word in itself! The term *panic attack*, however, takes it to a different level: it is, quite literally, an ATTACK OF PANIC. It couldn't get much worse, right? People describe it feeling like "going to hell and back over and over again", while others liken it to having a sort of breakdown.

Sometimes it feels as if there is not even a clear *reason* for having a panic attack. Such experiences make you feel powerless and out of control, and our lives, relationships, work, and hobbies all move to second place. As a result, our whole life can be ruled by panic and fear; what it might mean, and what might happen. Our survival switch has been flicked on and we do not know (and cannot easily figure out) how to turn it off again. We are stuck, and not in a good place.

The first thing to remember is: *you are not alone*. Not at all. A large number of people will experience at least one panic attack in their lives and many people will experience several (myself included).[1] We sometimes forget that anxiety is actually an entirely normal emotion and plays a really important role in keeping us functioning well. Indeed, experiencing anxiety along with other emotions means we are emotionally well-regulated. It's when our anxiety takes over to the exclusion of all other emotions that problems arise.

A large number of people will experience at least one panic attack in their lives and many people will experience several.

This is where I hope this book might be of help. In it, I will endeavour to give you a better understanding of your emotions, especially anxiety. I will explain how anxiety can manifest as panic attacks, their meaning and what you can do about them. The book aims to help you understand as well as develop a new relationship with your anxiety. A relationship of acceptance, that is empowering rather than limiting, that will allow you not only to get your life back, but perhaps make it more rewarding, since it will be based on a deeper and better knowledge of yourself and your emotions.

In that respect, having panic attacks creates an opportunity to understand and accept your emotions, which can be empowering and something of an advantage in life. Going through such experiences allows you not only to gain a deeper understanding of yourself, but also to further trust yourself and become emotionally stronger.

Your experiences allow you to gain a deeper understanding of yourself and become emotionally stronger.

Why I Wrote This Book

For some time now, I have been wanting to write about what I know concerning anxiety and panic attacks, what I have seen, and also what I have learned. I am a clinical psychologist and have been for over 20 years. Since very early on in my career I developed a deep interest in anxiety, what it means and how it works. I have worked in several clinical settings like psychiatric hospitals, student psychological support centres, charities, the NHS and also my own private practice. I became an anxiety specialist by focusing on anxiety-related difficulties during my training and then doing several extra post-graduation study courses that concentrated on understanding and treating anxiety disorders. Because I also always valued science and evidence for what works, what does not work, and why, I have also always worked in academic institutions, did a Master's degree, a PhD, and conducted research on anxiety. I am still passionate about this work and what I do.

I am interested in how anxiety, being such an important emotion, can also be so detrimental to someone's life. More importantly, I find it remarkable how people also overcome such difficulties and find the understanding and motivation to get back on track. Studying and working with people who have had these types of experiences and difficulties has made my work rewarding, and most of all, I have learnt so much about others, myself and how empowering it can be when we challenge ourselves.

Anxiety is such an important emotion,
but can also be so detrimental
to someone's life.

I remain eager to learn more about anxiety and to share with people that are either curious or experience such feelings, and I hope my experience, passion and work will also contribute to your understanding and help you in navigating your anxiety-related difficulties and panic attacks.

The Approach Used in This Book

I like to simplify. Experiencing and making sense of emotions is not always an easy task; it can be complex and overwhelming. The experience of a panic attack is frightening and not easy to understand, especially if we keep in perspective that when we feel highly anxious, we focus on protecting ourselves rather than understanding what is really happening. While feeling scared, a fight between our emotions and what we know seems to take place. I find it useful to think of it as a fight between two opposing armies. On one side is our army of knowledge and experience – our rational, decision-making mind. On the other is our army of sensations, feelings and emotions – irrational, unreasonable and frightening. In this war between what we know and what we feel, we sometimes do not know which side we should take; our feelings are just too powerful and overwhelming. While fearful and highly anxious, we will mostly have an urge to protect ourselves and survive, and will pay less attention to what we actually know. This happens automatically and is not something we are consciously aware of or can decide upon.

While feeling highly anxious and scared,
a fight between our emotions and what
we know seems to take place.

This book will show you what happens when you have a panic attack, by helping you understand the battle that takes place between your army of knowledge and your army of feelings. It describes how, if left unchecked, the influence of what you know (your army of knowledge) begins to weaken and how you start looking to your emotions, along with ways to escape and strategies to cope.

We'll explore how, eventually, you end up siding with your emotions and letting go of what you once knew, which means that on your personal battlefield, your feelings are winning the war, and are now so powerful that they will rule your actions. Your coping strategies are no longer successfully taking the pain and fear away; instead, they are taking your life away.

As well as trying to simplify and make sense of such knowledge vs feelings experience, this book will also uncover some of your secret weapons. It will show you how to fight your feelings more fairly by bringing what you know on to the battlefield.

The main goal of this book is therefore not only to increase your knowledge, but also to achieve a better relationship between your knowledge and feelings. To sign a peace treaty and to get your life back; a life that does not require avoidance, escape or coping strategies, as your feelings and knowledge will then be at peace. It will help you to reclaim your life and change it for the better.

How to Use This Book

The book takes you step by step toward understanding how you reached this battlefield in the first place, how you can find your new weapons, and how you can sign the peace treaty.

Chapter 1 explains what anxiety and panic attacks are, how common they are, and how people experience them. You will also learn to understand what signs might indicate a panic attack is taking place, identify what it feels like for you, and how feelings of panic may progress from being a normal experience to a potential problem. We will also explore what your main triggers for panic attacks are.

Chapter 2 will help you understand the physiology of fear, anxiety and panic. This chapter puts your panic attacks into context, explaining the function they serve for our welfare as human beings. We will discover that our interpretation of the sensations of a panic attack we experience can either heighten the attack or lessen its impact.

Chapter 3 will help you understand your response to your panic attack – the behaviours which you instinctively put in place to cope with or attempt to prevent further panic attacks altogether. We will explore whether such behaviours are effective or beneficial and unearth any patterns in this behaviour.

In Chapter 4 you will work to develop a more positive coping strategy when a panic attack hits. First, by acknowledging the importance of not being alone in your issues, seeking support and reaching out to your family and friends. And then, by addressing the situations during which panic attacks seem to commonly occur. The chapter will arm you with ways of changing your perspective on panic and looking at it differently. Through this chapter, you will be challenged to try to accept your feelings, and minimize the coping strategies you utilize.

You will be challenged to try to accept your feelings, and minimize your coping strategies.

Finally, Chapter 5 brings to the picture the importance of self-care and explores how panic attacks might make self-care difficult. This chapter will introduce some ideas on how to improve self-care and work toward acceptance, looking for a better management of anxiety and panic-attack-related difficulties, as well as showing how empowering it can be to further understand yourself and your anxiety.

How To Use the Exercises in This Book

To win wars we need knowledge, strategies, weapons and practice. To increase your chances of a fair fight, the book provides a number of exercises that will allow you to acquire these things. You are encouraged to engage with the information you have read and adapt it to your own experiences.

Gaining knowledge, developing and practising strategies, and picking the right weapons are not always straightforward processes or easy tasks, and some exercises can be more challenging than others. Motivation is key, so I hope you are motivated to give it a try and I urge you to treat yourself with compassion as you attempt these.

There are no rights or wrongs; the exercises are not part of an exam process; they are part of a learning process, realizing what you already know, identifying your strengths, acquiring new knowledge and understanding your feelings. Be kind to yourself, as everything you do takes you a step forward, to learn more and to feel empowered to stand on the battlefield.

There are no rights or wrongs; the exercises will help identify your strengths, acquire new knowledge and understand your feelings.

It may help to use a specific notebook to document your journey through this book. We will refer back to previous exercises as we gain a greater picture of your experience of panic attacks and the specific strategies that may help you.

Author Notes

Throughout this book, you will find several examples that illustrate panic attacks and peoples' experiences with them. During my career, I have worked with many people experiencing panic attacks and the examples herein are based on their journey to not only understand but also to change their experience. Their stories and names are fictional for confidentiality reasons.

Please note: this book is not a scientific one. It is based on my clinical experience and the knowledge gained in my academic work, and is therefore grounded in scientific research and evidence-based practice, but you don't need a background in medicine or science to read and understand its contents.

Before moving forward and starting on this journey together, I wish you the very best of luck. I hope this works for you and that, as we go along, you start to feel more empowered and gain a greater knowledge of who you are, of what you can achieve, and begin to trust in your ability to handle your life no matter how you feel. I will be with you every step of the way.

CHAPTER 1

DOES PANIC RULE YOUR LIFE?

What is a Panic Attack?

Panic attacks have been described in medical and scientific literature for many years, and some reports date from as early as the 16th century. However, only relatively recently have they been given the attention they deserve.

In the 1980s, science and medicine started not only to acknowledge but also to understand panic attacks. Around the same time, anxiety in general became a strong area of interest. Knowledge was gradually acquired, and, after several decades of research and investment into understanding panic attacks both from a biological and psychological perspective, a definition emerged.

The most recent definition can be found in the *Diagnostic and Statistical Manual for of Mental Disorders-5* (DSM–5), which contains most mental-health-related problems and is used by psychologists, psychiatrists and doctors. In it, a panic attack is defined as "An abrupt surge of intense fear or intense discomfort that reaches a peak within minutes."[2]

A panic attack is "An abrupt surge of intense fear
or intense discomfort that reaches
a peak within minutes."

During a panic attack, four or more of the following symptoms occur:

- Palpitations, pounding heart, or accelerated heart rate
- Sweating
- Trembling or shaking
- Feelings of choking
- Nausea or abdominal distress
- Chills or heat sensations
- Derealization (feelings of unreality) or depersonalization (feeling detached from oneself)
- Sensations of shortness of breath or smothering
- Chest pain or discomfort
- Feeling dizzy, unsteady, light-headed or faint
- Fear of losing control or "going crazy"
- Paraesthesia (numbness or tingling sensations)
- Fear of dying

From the list above, you can see that the symptoms can be both *cognitive* (thoughts) and *physical* (bodily sensations).

Generally, as the manual states, four symptoms are required to call such distressing experiences a panic attack. If the experience consists of fewer than four symptoms, such episodes are called "limited symptoms panic attacks" (which nonetheless are still worrying and devastating for those experiencing them).

Importantly, to be considered a panic attack, these feelings should not be caused by an obviously life-threatening situation. So, for example, if you are driving 200 miles per hour and feel panic about having an accident, that would not be considered a panic attack, as those feelings are related to a scenario that contains real danger.

It is worth noting at this point that the cognitive symptoms (thoughts), such as fear of dying, losing control, or "going crazy", are informal terms used by people to describe their experiences, and are not used as diagnostic terms or as any form of judgement.

A broad range of other symptoms can also be present, although they are not common for most people. Some examples are:

- A dry mouth
- Headaches
- Crying
- Screaming
- Tinnitus (ringing in the ears)
- Muscle aches and pains (e.g. a sore neck)

How a Panic Attack is Different from Anxiety

When a panic attack takes place, it is severe, distinct and reaches its hardest point (or peak) within minutes. This is where it differs from general anxiety. For example, people can describe feeling anxious for the whole day and then experiencing a panic attack, but also feeling anxious for a whole day and not experiencing panic attacks.

What is it Like to Have a Panic Attack?

Panic attacks might build, starting with initial feelings of mild apprehension or uneasiness, but can also come on quite suddenly, with no warning or notice. They may not even be associated with any particular or obvious cause.

The experience seems to be broadly the same for most people, although you and I might describe it in different ways because we are all more sensitive to or dislike particular sensations, in which case those are likely to be the ones we remember and focus on the most. You might feel your heart racing or notice changes in your breathing, then you might feel shaky and sweaty. I, however, might feel spaced out, dizzy or have cold sweats and nausea. Either way, these feelings have one thing in common: they are all deeply unpleasant. You might feel like you are going to have a heart attack, are about to faint, be sick, lose control or even die. It feels real; it feels like *it is just about to happen*.

What do these feelings mean? Why are they happening? What is *wrong*? These are all logical questions, for which you cannot usually find a logical answer.

Understandably, you might come to fear having a panic attack and all the horrible sensations that come with it. It is no exaggeration to say that panic attacks can have a devastating effect on our mental health and wellbeing. Sometimes, after experiencing one or more panic attacks, your life can become almost unrecognizable. Suddenly you find yourself walking, not your chosen path, but one determined by fear and survival. You no longer look at the world around you in the same way, or look at what your relationships normally have to offer you.

Instead, you start focusing on yourself, on what you feel or might feel, on avoiding panic attacks and the sensations that come with them. You dedicate serious time thinking what could be dangerous and therefore start a panic attack. Your actions are now determined by what *could* be, and what *might* happen is never positive; it is frightening and catastrophic. Your life is now ruled by the fear of losing control or even dying. You are no longer the self you recognize, and your confidence takes a hit.

If you experience panic attacks regularly,
your actions become determined by what *could* be,
and what *might* happen.

After a while, you start finding ways of actively preventing something bad from happening, and you do so by creating coping mechanisms – also called "protective behaviours". We will look closely at these behaviours in Chapter 3. As this continues, you also develop *a fear of fear.* That's right: you are constantly *fearful* of *feeling fear*!

EXERCISE: Identify the Sensations of Your Panic Attacks

I suggest you begin documenting your journey in a notebook and start to adapt and relate what you have read so far to your own experience.

Think about the physical sensations you experience during a panic attack. Which ones are you able to identify?

Have a look through the lists on pages 14–15 and note which of the main symptoms you experience in your notebook or journal.

Make sure you include all of them and highlight the most common and the most threatening ones using the table below as a template.

For each sensation, write down why you do not like it, what it means for you, and what you think could happen when you experience it. For example:

Physical sensations	Why I don't like it/What it means/What could happen
e.g. nausea	Makes me feel sick, I need to make sure I don't vomit, I will vomit, will lose control and it will be awful

This exercise is important. It is the first step to start understanding your own experience with panic.

I believe we cannot really change anything we do not understand and identifying your own experience is fundamental.

You have now identified the physical sensations that are frightening to you and which you struggle with. They are not pleasant, and probably feel harmful and terrifying.

We will refer back to this exercise when discussing the importance of how you interpret your panic attacks on page 54.

What Can Trigger Panic Attacks?

Just as everyone experiences panic attacks differently, what might cause one to come about varies from person to person. You might have panic attacks at seemingly random times, completely out of the blue. Some people describe restless nights and remember experiencing panic-like sensations during sleep. Others wake up while experiencing such symptoms. Some people experience panic attacks while being active or doing other activities (watching TV, drinking, or using drugs, for example), while panic attacks can also happen to others when they are in specific situations or places (like driving, heights, shops, escalators, while with animals, etc).

As well as particular **situations and places**, panic attacks can be triggered by specific **physical sensations**, feelings of **anticipation,** or by having **thoughts about panic attacks**.

Situations and Places

Some people seem to be more vulnerable to experiencing panic attacks in particular situations and places. For example:

- Feeling trapped somewhere (e.g. in a lift, cinema, train, aeroplane, etc.)
- Receiving bad news
- Having an argument with someone
- Experiencing a major life change
- Witnessing others experiencing difficult situations
- Being in particularly "stressful" places (whatever that means to you) (e.g. shops, queues, crowed places, etc.)
- Being alone

Physical Sensations

For some people, panic attacks are brought on by noticing physical symptoms or feeling certain bodily sensations. For example, feeling your heart race can trigger the fear of having a heart attack, or feeling dizzy might make you afraid of fainting.

Anticipation

Panic attacks can also take place when *anticipating* events, situations, or things going wrong (like a public presentation, doing an exam at school or university, having surgery, going to the dentist, or even going out for dinner with friends). Even the anticipation of further panic attacks can be a trigger for such episodes.

Thoughts About Panic

Thinking about panic or panic attacks can also be a trigger in itself. For some people thinking, talking, or even hearing about panic attacks can trigger such episodes. I have worked with clients that found it difficult to even describe their experiences with anxiety and panic. Sometimes they needed breaks when telling me about it.

Individual Experiences

Let's look at some examples of how others experience panic, and what their triggers may be. Notice if any of their experiences resonate with you.

Alfred was triggered by a situation most of us have faced while travelling:

"I was commuting on the London underground and the driver said we would be stopping at a red light for a while. I felt uneasy and trapped, but there was no escape. I felt my heart racing, and I kept checking my pulse. It was going fast, really fast. It was getting faster. I tried to control my breathing and calm down."

Thea was shopping for a dress to wear to a wedding when she started feeling hot and sweaty, then nauseous:

"My mouth was dry. Everything started bothering me, the lights, the racks with clothes, people's faces and anything and everything. I picked a dress and decided not to try it, just went to pay. I was now really sweaty, shaking, my mouth was dry, I had palpitations and felt like I couldn't breathe. I felt like I was detaching from my body and felt a sense of disconnection. It was horrible."

Aisha was at work when she suddenly noticed her heart racing:

"It got stronger and I thought something was wrong with me. I sat down and started monitoring myself. It wouldn't stop, I was breathing fast and getting sweaty and started to feel pain in my arm. I thought I was going to have a heart attack, I asked for help. My manager called an ambulance and I went to hospital."

For Sophia, there was seemingly no reason at all for her panic attack:

> *"That day I was cooking, which I find relaxing, and also kind of daydreaming. Out of the blue I notice myself crying, my heart was racing and my chest was tight, I was breathing really fast and could hardly catch my breath. My mouth was dry, my legs felt really weak, I was dizzy and felt hot and cold."*

Although different, there is a common pattern to these experiences. Each involves:

- physical sensations that are sudden, uncomfortable and unpleasant
- thoughts about something threatening happening
- attempts to cope or escape

For some, there is also a new way of living compromised by the concern or fear of experiencing another panic attack.

Tom had a panic attack while being asked by his family about his plans for the future. Now he avoids all forms of confrontation.

> *"The problem is, now I don't like to talk with anyone that is my superior or I admire. I feel like if anything gets argumentative, I will have a panic attack."*

The variety in the experience of these distressing episodes does not stop there. Panic attacks can arrive while you are feeling calm and relaxed (as with Sophia) *or* while you are feeling anxious (as with Alfred). If they arrive while you are feeling anxious, although the anxiety was there already, the panic attack starts with a sudden feeling of discomfort. After such a difficult experience is over, you may feel as before; anxious or calm.

Expected or Unexpected

Panic attacks can be described as expected or unexpected:

- When a panic attack occurs due to a clear or obvious sign or trigger (i.e. a situation during which a panic attack normally takes place) it is considered an *expected panic attack*.
- When a panic attack occurs *without* a clear or obvious cue or trigger, it is considered an *unexpected panic attack*. For example, some people wake up from sleep while having a panic attack, in which case they are experiencing an unexpected nocturnal panic attack.

Research has shown that expected panic attacks occur three to four times more often than unexpected panic attacks.[3]

EXERCISE: Identify Your Triggers

Recognizing what your triggers are is another important step toward gaining a full understanding of what the experience of panic is like for you. Record this exercise in your notebook.

What triggers your army of feelings? Is it a particular situation or place? Is it a particular physical sensation? Is it the anticipation of events or situations? A thought? Or all of them?

Write down as many triggers as you can identify. There are no rights or wrongs; it is all about you, and your experience is unique.

After identifying your triggers, write down (as shown in the example table below) what you think might happen if you were in that situation or while anticipating it, or when experiencing the physical sensations.

Trigger	What might happen if I am in that situation
e.g. being on a train stuck in a tunnel	It might stop, I will not be able to leave, I won't be able to breathe and will faint.
e.g. being in a crowded shop	It is crowded, I feel trapped, I will lose control.

This exercise is important. You are another step further on your journey to understanding your own experience with panic.

You have now identified how panic physically manifests for you (in the previous exercise on page 18) and now what your triggers are.

Your army of knowledge is getting more prepared to start facing the idea of challenging your army of feelings. We will refer back to this exercise later.

How Common Are Panic Attacks?

It may help you to know that to experience panic attacks is very common. They seem to be more prevalent in females than in males, but the way in which they manifest, their signs and triggers, is the same regardless of your gender. A recent study performed in 25 countries found that 13.3% of people will have a panic attack at some point in their life.[4]

13.3% of people will have a panic attack at some point in their life.

The same study found that there were certain circumstances that seemed to be more frequently associated with the experience of panic attacks, including:

- being under the age of 60
- being a young adult
- being unemployed or disabled
- being divorced/separated/widowed
- having lower education or household income

Panic attacks can also be associated with some medical conditions, such as cardiac, respiratory, vestibular, and gastrointestinal health problems, as well as many other mental health problems, such as:

- anxiety-related difficulties (panic disorder, social anxiety, health anxiety, obsessive compulsive disorder, post-traumatic stress disorder, specific phobia, and generalised anxiety disorder)
- mood-related difficulties (depression, bipolar disorder)
- eating disorders
- personality disorders
- psychotic disorders
- substance-use disorders

Recurrent Panic Attacks

Panic attacks are not pleasant and can be serious, especially if they become frequent. For two thirds of the people who experience a single panic attack, such episodes became recurrent. This is especially worrying because panic attacks have been associated with a higher rate of suicide attempts and suicidal ideation (thoughts about suicide), even when other difficulties and other suicide risk factors are taken into consideration.[5] If you have suicidal thoughts, please seek help. Refer to the Useful Resources section at the back of the book for more information.

For two thirds of people who experience a single panic attack, such episodes become recurrent.

It is, therefore, first and foremost, crucial to understand what is going on when you have a panic attack. To know what is actually happening, in your body and your mind, and what it all means. Once you have that understanding, you can build on that to figure out what to do about them, start taking obstacles out of the way and finally get your life back.

Knowledge vs Feelings

Remember that fight I spoke about in the introduction? The war between the two armies of what you *know* and what you *feel*? Well, it is time for that war to be over!

You need your army of knowledge to win over the army of feelings that is currently controlling you. Then, what you really need is for them to sign a peace treaty and get back to existing in a mutual relationship – a co-operation, a friendship.

First, though, we need to understand what we're dealing with.

CHAPTER 2

UNDERSTANDING FEAR AND ANXIETY

To understand what is actually happening when you have a panic attack, it is important to first understand what *fear* and *anxiety* are. Secondly, we must appreciate how these emotions affect how we feel *physically* and how we *think*.

From the examples in the previous chapter, it is clear that people feel specific physical sensations when experiencing fear and/or anxiety, and also have associated thoughts that are catastrophic in nature most of the time.

For years, researchers have focused on trying to understand if fear and anxiety are indeed different emotions. There are many aspects to consider when making a distinction between the two, and even today the difference is still not fully understood. Nonetheless, broadly speaking:

- **Fear** can be described as an emotion that we experience as a result of a survival response to threat, and it occurs when a threat is *present* or *imminent.*
- **Anxiety**, on the other hand, concerns a threat that is not present but *possible* and *anticipated* and its occurrence is *uncertain.*

In other words, the difference is in the timing: fear is about what is happening *right now*, whereas anxiety is about what *might* happen in the future.

Fear is about what is happening *right now*,
whereas anxiety is about what *might*
happen in the future.

Understanding Fear and the "Fight or Flight" Response

Let's imagine you decide to have a break from your
busy life and visit the park or a nature reserve. You are
enjoying your walk when, suddenly, a bear comes out of
the woods. What do you feel at that point in time? That's
right: fear!

Now, when faced with a threat such as this, as a human
being – whether you want to or not – you will prioritize
your survival over everything else, and your brain and
body will do this without waiting to ask for permission. As
a result, you will be in what's called "fight or flight mode",
which initially means your body experiences a rush of the
hormone adrenaline. Why? Well, whether we decide we are
more likely to survive this situation by engaging physically
with the bear (fight) or getting as far away from it as we
can (flight), we don't have time to indulge in the privilege of
warming up, stretching our muscles or generally preparing
the body for what it is about to face. Instead, we need our
muscles to be ready to fight or run in a split second, and
that is where adrenaline comes in; it speeds up the process

of being ready for action. This bodily response happens for a reason: to protect us, which of course our bodies are designed to do.

Bodily responses happen for a reason:
to protect us.

So, in order to fight or run, our muscles need to be fully functional. To do that, they need oxygen, which is carried by blood. Because of this we will feel differences in our breathing patterns. To make sure we have enough oxygen coming in, breathing becomes faster and usually deeper, the heart starts pumping harder and faster to make sure that oxygen is carried in our blood to the muscles via our blood vessels at an optimal rate (which can cause palpitations, a heavy chest or chest pain). Consequently, our blood pressure increases and we might feel dizzy or spaced out (due to the changes in oxygen supply to the brain).

Because our survival depends on them, our muscles take priority over everything else going on in the body. In short, if a process in the body is not useful for fighting or running away from the bear (or whatever causes you to go into survival mode), the brain will not make it a priority and might stop it or slow it down. This means that our digestion slows down and saliva production reduces (since eating a meal is not on the agenda), the bladder relaxes (we do not yet have a clear explanation for this but there are some ideas that suggest voiding might be an advantage for further action), and less blood flow reaches the surface of our skin (because it is concentrating in the muscles), among many others. Each of these changes in the body causes physical sensations to occur. These are part of our innate survival response, and are listed in the table below.

Bodily process	Physical sensation
The heart pumps faster to deliver oxygen-rich blood to the muscles	Heart racing or palpitations
The lungs need more oxygen, which will then be carried by the blood supply	Breathing changes
Your body attempts to maintain an appropriate body temperature	Shaking, sweating, hot or cold sensations
Differences in oxygen concentration and supply to the brain	Dizziness, derealization (feelings of unreality), depersonalization (feeling detached from oneself)
Less blood affluence to stomach (as digestion is not a priority)	Nausea

Bodily process	Physical sensation
Less blood to the surface of the skin and to fingers and toes to prioritize muscles and also more oxygen carried in the blood than usual	Numbness and tingling
Less saliva production (as digestive processes are no longer a priority)	Dry mouth, dry throat
Tension in neck area muscles	Tight throat
The chest tightening to allow changes in breathing and more oxygen consumption	Chest pain or discomfort
Less blood to the surface of the skin	Paleness
Bladder and bowels relaxing (voiding possibly further prepares body for action)	Urge to go the bathroom

All of these responses – the heart beating faster, the lungs taking in more air, and other similar responses – are initiated in a split second. And, as if it wasn't clever enough, we now know that our brain does all of this before we are even consciously aware of it. What do I mean by that?

Imagine you are walking along a street, either looking at your phone, talking on the phone, talking to someone walking with you, or even just thinking about what to cook for dinner. What you are *not* thinking about is if there are any holes or unevenness in the floor that you need to be aware of. And that's because your brain sends messages to your body to make adjustments in your walking pattern without you having to think about it consciously. When you cross a road while talking to your friend, you do not deliberately stop and think, *Now I need to look right or left to see if there is traffic coming*. You just do it. Just like that. Automatically. It sounds like such a simple thing, but in fact your brain has worked hard all your life to make sure that running on "auto-pilot" like this is possible.

Through our senses, our brain constantly receives information. That information allows the brain to make decisions, without us ever being aware of them.

Through our main senses (touch, sight, hearing, smell and taste, and the sense of space or proprioception), and also more subtle senses (like movements to control balance, etc.), our brain constantly receives information. That information allows the brain to make decisions, without us ever being aware of them. In order to be able to react to things very quickly, if necessary, some of that information is analysed in a fast and not very detailed manner. That is what happens with information that is associated with some sort of threat or danger. If you are walking and your eyes detect a hole in the pavement, your brain will initiate a sequence of events to make you walk in a way so that you do not fall and hurt yourself (with varying degrees of success, as anyone who's ever suffered the mortifying experience of taking a tumble in the middle of the street will know…). As you walk, you did not really consciously think about avoiding the obstacle; you were only aware that you were walking over the hole or moving around it (if you even consciously thought about it at all).

Going back to the bear emerging from the woods analogy, when your brain receives the information via your eyes, it is immediately sent to the more primal areas of the brain, such as those dealing with attention (the thalamus) and threat (the amygdala). If what you spotted is threat-related, a survival response (that adrenaline rush) is immediately initiated. This all happens before any conscious awareness on your part. That information is then compared with your stored memories (which happens in the hippocampus area of the brain), and if it confirms that the possibly threat-related information is actually a truly dangerous situation, the brain will increase the activation of the fear-related brain network (because it involves several areas) and the fight or flight response will be fully established and ongoing. All of this becomes conscious only when we decide to do something about it. You might decide to run away from the bear, but, in fact, your body was already ready to run or fight before you made that decision.

If the bear wanders away, the threat goes away and you do not need to do anything, so your body goes back to normal.

Either way, what was always conscious to you was your experience of fear, meaning what you *actually felt*. You are experiencing fear, and as far as your conscious awareness of it goes, to experience fear is to know that you are in danger. Your emotions are the feelings you experience when you consciously acknowledge the consequences of such danger.

You are experiencing fear, and as far as your conscious awareness of it goes, to experience fear is to know that you are in danger.

Our body's way of responding to threats, which is more a reflex than a conscious decision, has been advantageous throughout evolution. These survival mechanisms have an ancient evolutionary origin, and in fact many other animals show very similar responses, with similar brain circuits that control them. If you think about it, it makes sense that animals that had efficient fight or flight (fear) responses many millions of years ago were less likely to be eaten by predators. That means they were more likely to survive, to reproduce, and to pass those efficient responses on to their offspring. These responses and the brain machinery that control them have been preserved and passed down over millions of years of evolution to us. And even though we are very unlikely to be eaten by a bear in the modern world, these responses are still with us, hard-wired into our DNA and our brain chemistry.

Even though we are very unlikely to be eaten
by a bear in the modern world, our threat response
is still with us, hard-wired into our DNA
and our brain chemistry.

Understanding Anxiety

So that was fear, but what about its partner – anxiety? Perhaps the best way to explain it is to go back to the example of the bear emerging from the woods. Imagine a week has gone by since that truly frightening encounter and you decide to go for another walk. You are enjoying the breeze and sunshine, when suddenly you become apprehensive; you feel uncomfortable, and begin to have what feels like a fight or flight response. But there's no bear to be seen. Why is this happening?

You guessed right; you remember what happened the last time you went for a walk. You are anticipating the appearance of the bear. You are (understandably) anxious about such a possibility, wondering when/if it might happen. The problem is, bear or no bear, our brain is going to respond no matter what. You've anticipated a threat, so, just in case, it will initiate a fight or flight response. Now, it is also important to note that this experience also brings about certain emotions. In this case, the emotion is anxiety. You are anxious about what *might* happen next and your experience of the anxiety will also *influence* or *determine* what happens next.

Anxiety is a future-oriented emotion that involves a sense of uncontrollability and unpredictability over potential anticipated threats. The person experiencing anxiety as an emotion focuses their attention on potential threats or threatening situations and on their own ability to cope or respond effectively to such threats or situations.

Anxiety is a future-oriented emotion that involves a sense of uncontrollability and unpredictability over potential anticipated threats.

Past Experiences

Alongside all the processes we have been talking about is our brain's ability to learn, to store knowledge in our memory. We continuously learn throughout our lives, and our decisions (both unconscious and conscious) are dependent on such ongoing learning. For one, it means we are able to use our personal past experiences to make predictions about the future. (Something else we can thank evolution for.)

For example, imagine that you were never scared of bees – in fact, you always saw them as an important part of the natural world and actually thought they were quite beautiful. Then comes the day when you are stung by one. It was not pleasant and you had a rather bad experience. Your brain has now learned that *bees are dangerous*, and from then on it is not only able to enter survival mode if you hear or spot a bee, but also to *anticipate* that there will likely be bees around if you visit gardens or parks.

As we've seen, an important characteristic of anxiety is uncertainty; uncertainty about danger and where or when it will occur. With that in mind, it's easy to understand that there is uncertainty also about the *duration* of such danger (e.g. how long will the bee be around me? How long will I be in pain if it stings me?), and what should be done to either cope or prevent it from happening in the first place.

It's easy to understand that there is uncertainty about the *duration* of perceived danger, and what should be done to either cope or prevent it from happening.

The relationship between learning and memory is also a very personal one. Each of us will develop a unique memory of a particular experience (of being stung by a bee, for example), which means each of us will have different experiences and approaches to uncertainty, anticipation and anxiety. This is because such memories depend not only on *what* and *how* something happened, but also on *when* – and *when* things happened also has important links to other events in your life.

Even if there seems to be no apparent reason for a panic attack, there is always *something* triggering such episodes.

This means that even if there seems to be no apparent reason for a panic attack, there is always *something* triggering such episodes, and the reason might lay in previous experiences that have occurred in your life some time before, which have been learned and stored in your memory. Stressful situations in life tend to have a great emotional impact on us. These could be related to your own or someone in your family's health, relationship problems, big changes in life, accidents, financial issues, or work-related difficulties, and although such situations might no longer be present when you experience your first panic attack, they have had an impact on you.

It might be the case that, when you had your first panic attack, you were feeling more vulnerable because of those experiences, could finally relax after an exhausting life period, or there was a small trigger that brought everything rushing back.

The reason for your panic attacks might lie in previous experiences that have occurred in your life some time before, which have been learned and stored in your memory.

At the time of writing, the world is suffering through the COVID-19 pandemic. I do not think it would be at all surprising if, after the pandemic, many people start experiencing panic attacks as they try to get their lives back to normal.

EXERCISE: Identify Stressful or Difficult Experiences From Your Past

Our experiences shape who we are and contribute greatly to the way we see and interact with the world. They are important to understand why we react to difficult or fearful situations in particular ways or even why some of us tend to engage in anticipation more than others.

To take one more step toward the understanding of your own experience of panic attacks, identify experiences from your past that were stressful, difficult or during which you were scared or anxious and record these in your notebook. For example:

- *"My first panic attack came after I was made redundant."*
- *"As my relationship broke down, I noticed I was having more panic attacks."*
- *"My panic attacks seemed to worsen when I went back to work after sick leave."*

Combined with the previous exercises, you have now identified:

- your physical sensations during a panic attack
- what triggers such episodes

- how these might be related to your life experiences

You are forming a picture of your panic attacks, and are arming yourself with information to move on to address them.

Your Response to Perceived Threat

As previously described, feeling fear and anxiety is a normal and ingrained consequence of the survival response that is so crucial to us as human beings. You experience those unpleasant feelings listed on page 14 because you are designed that way to respond to threats. However, it might seem more understandable and less unpleasant if we were to only have such experiences when the stimulus was present. So, when the bear emerges from the woods, you would rightly view the feelings and sensations created by the subsequent fight or flight response as quite normal, not as a panic attack, even though you might say that you "panicked". On the other hand, if there was no bear and you still had that survival response, the odds are that you would think something has gone wrong and interpret your panic in a rather catastrophic and illogical way. Nonetheless, your reaction *is* logical; it *is* frightening and really feels like something *is* wrong. Once more, you are not alone, and it makes sense to see your reaction in that way.

Your reaction to perceived threat is logical,
and it makes sense to react that way.

When you experience feelings of fear and anxiety, you will respond by behaving in particular ways. Some of these are part of the unconscious fear detection and survival response (e.g. breathing deeper and faster), and some part of a more conscious process that is related to your experience of fear, what you feel and what you do when you consciously reason and make decisions (e.g. breathing slowly to control your breathing). These more conscious processes and decisions are what influence and trigger further fear and anxiety responses. These are what we are interested in exploring in this book, and what we can change.

For example, imagine you are travelling on the train. You commute to work on a daily basis, but today is different. The train stops, and an announcement is made that it will be stationary in a tunnel for an uncertain amount of time. You are in a rush and have an important meeting that day, that your job depends on. Needless to say, you do not like the announcement.

Your experience may play out as described opposite, which also shows how your brain is responding to the perceived threat.

Your experience	What's really going on
Suddenly your heart is racing, your breathing is faster, you have sweaty palms and feel dizzy.	Your brain has identified a threat and initiated a fight or flight response.
You think you are going to collapse or faint.	You have become conscious of your experience of fear and are making interpretations of such feelings.
Your heart races even faster, you are sweating all over, trembling, dizzy and have wobbly legs.	Your brain is now dealing with another threat: your belief that you will either collapse or faint.
You feel awful and worry about what will happen when you faint. It will be embarrassing and no one will help you.	You are interpreting your experience further and making assumptions based on your emotions.
You feel anxious, terrified.	Your brain continues in fight or flight mode as it senses that a threat is imminent.
You sit by the aisle, near the exit, to be ready to make a quick escape. You look for some water.	Your brain initiates behaviours to try to help you escape the situation.
You try to reassure yourself that you are sitting by the exit, the train will move soon and you will get out at the following station.	Your brain has learned that something bad would happen if you did not change seats.

Your experience	What's really going on
Nonetheless, you are still anxious and fearful.	Your behaviours add or maintain your feelings, which only confirms your interpretation.
The train starts finally moving, you feel relieved and get off at the next stop.	Your brain moves toward getting you back to normal.

Why Can a Rational Response Feel So Irrational?

As we have been discussing, panic attacks are characterized by a sudden, strong physiological (bodily) activation that is associated with perceptions of imminent threat or danger (e.g. fainting, losing control, having a heart attack or even dying).

After a panic attack, some people admit that they think the situation was not as dangerous as it seemed or they anticipated, and that their experience was somewhat exaggerated. But they also say that it was impossible for them to inhibit the fear reaction in the situation.

Again, it all goes back to that fight between what you *know* and what you *feel*. Your army of knowledge might somehow understand that you are not in as much danger as you feel; there is no bear, the train stopping is a totally normal occurrence. Your army of knowledge *knows* this and is trying to voice it loudly. However, your army of feelings is doing what it does best: making you feel things. As we've seen, these feelings are unusual, unpleasant and cause you to be highly focused on yourself and your body, which means you silence everything else – including your army of knowledge. And so, you listen, focus and interpret the sensations as if something must be wrong. Sometimes seriously wrong.

Your army of feelings are unpleasant and cause you to be highly focused on yourself and your body, which means you silence everything else - including your army of knowledge.

Then, even after the situation passes, you remember how awful it was; you never want to experience something like that again. Once more, your army of feelings is given more power than your army of knowledge. Even though you *know* that nothing was actually wrong, it doesn't matter – your feelings win out and all you remember is that it felt bad. *Really* bad.

Your Interpretation is Key

As mentioned earlier, your interpretation of a situation is dependent on your past history and experiences, i.e. what has been stored in your memory. As a result of your first panic attack, you are now fearful of your own body and sensations. You are fearful of fear. You are interpreting totally normal situations and sensations as incredibly threatening. Unfortunately, the fact that you really *believe* they are, means that the resulting emotions are not only logical, but just as real as if the situation or sensation really was something to be feared. Although it might feel irrational (because the danger is not real), there is nothing wrong with you. Your body is doing its job in an exemplary manner; it is protecting you. However, because it is protecting you from an absent danger, it feels awful, irrational, uncontrollable and unpredictable.

Although it might feel irrational (because the danger is not real), there is nothing wrong with you. Your body is doing its job in an exemplary manner; it is protecting you.

For example, while experiencing heart palpitations, some people think they are about to have a heart attack. Or, if they're feeling dizzy, that they will collapse or faint. This belief may not make sense, and danger might not be present, but the awful sensations are there, and our search for an explanation is normal human behaviour. The interpretation is terrifying, and so fear and anxiety become the overruling emotions.

Below you will find some examples of physical sensations and interpretations often reported by people that experience panic attacks.

Sensations	Possible interpretation
Heart racing or palpitations	I am going to have a heart attack
Breathing changes	I am suffocating, I cannot breathe
Shaking	There is something wrong with me
Sweating	I am going to lose control, I am going to panic
Dizziness	I am going to faint or collapse
Nausea	I am going to vomit
Numbness and tingling	I am going to pass out
Derealization (feelings of unreality)	I am losing control
Depersonalization (feeling detached from oneself)	I am going crazy
Tight and/or dry throat	I am going to choke
Chest pain or discomfort	There is something wrong with my heart
Hot or cold sensations	I am going to pass out
Urge to go the bathroom	I am going to wet myself

EXERCISE: Identify Your Interpretation of the Sensations You Experience

Your thoughts and interpretations are another crucial step toward the knowledge you need to fight your army of feelings.

Refer back to the physical sensations you identified in the first exercise (page 18) and listed in your notebook. Add any that might be missing.

Now, using the information in this chapter, note down the bodily process that is involved in each of the physical sensations and add how you actually interpret the situation. See the table below for an example.

Physical sensation	Bodily process	My interpretation of what is happening
e.g. heart palpitations	*The heart pumps faster to deliver oxygen-rich blood to the muscles*	*I am going to have a heart attack*

Your army of knowledge now has further information to start making sense of the process involved in panic attacks and is therefore gaining strength relative to your army of feelings.

Well done for achieving these steps so far. We will refer back to this exercise later.

What Panic Attacks Do *Not* Mean

Taking into account the complex thoughts that panic brings into your life, there is much that needs clarifying. So, at this point I would like to empower your army of knowledge even further, with the information of what panic attacks do *not* mean.

As discussed previously, panic attacks are interpreted mostly in catastrophic ways because of the intense and painful sensations that accompany them. Some of the most common interpretations are the occurrence of a heart attack, losing consciousness or fainting, not being able to breathe or suffocating, choking, going crazy, losing control and dying. These can be enormously powerful feelings, but they are assumptions and interpretations, not facts. In reality, *panic does not lead to any of those outcomes*. The physical sensations experienced are real, but the interpretation is not. Don't believe me? Let's go through each of these examples and give your army of knowledge a boost.

They physical sensations of a panic attack are real,
but the interpretation is not.

"I'm going to have a heart attack"

Heart attacks do not occur because of the experience
of a panic attack. Heart attacks are caused by a
sudden interruption of the blood supply to the
heart. In a panic attack the supply is not interrupted
but increased. The pain and sensations reported
by people experiencing panic attacks is also rather
different from the pain that people with cardiovascular
problems report.

If panic attacks happen to people with heart problems,
or, indeed, other medical conditions, it is still possible to
understand which feelings are anxiety-related and which
are not, although caution is necessary to determine how to
understand the circumstances for that specific person and a
medical assessment is recommended.

"I'm going to pass out"

People simply cannot pass out or faint during a panic attack.
The straightforward reason for this is that, during a panic
attack, the blood pressure is high, and fainting is caused by
low blood pressure.

Fainting does not just happen, and if someone believes that it really does and that they *have* fainted as a result of a panic attack, some other factors need to be considered. For example, the fainting may have been caused by being unwell, sleep deprivation, food poisoning, a hangover, a virus, low blood pressure, or anaemia.

The only anxiety-related difficulty that can cause fainting is a blood, injection or injury phobia. In such cases, the sight of blood, having injections or seeing injuries can cause a sudden decrease in blood pressure, which in turn causes fainting.

You cannot faint during a panic attack as your blood pressure is high, and fainting is caused by low blood pressure.

"I can't breathe"

Not being able to breathe or suffocating is also not a possibility while having a panic attack. In fact, your body's goal is to breathe in *more* oxygen, which causes unpleasant sensations for some people. Some feel that their breathing is faster while others think that it is shallower. Both sensations are normal and part of the same physiological process (see page 35).

"I am going to choke"

Choking also does not occur. Feeling different sensations in your throat is caused by muscles tensing as part of the physiological fear response, as is dry mouth and difficulties swallowing due to less saliva production (see page 35). You do not need to worried about choking, therefore, as all of these sensations are normal.

"I am going crazy"

Although some of the physical sensations such as derealization and depersonalization (among others) might suggest that you are "going crazy", panic attacks do not cause those kinds of mental issues. Mental problems associated with being less lucid are very different to suffering from panic attacks, which are a normal response of the body. For people that experience them out of the blue and frequently, they might feel irrational and "crazy", but just because the body has an alarm response that occurs more often than required, that does not mean there is something wrong with your sanity. It only means that the emotions need to be understood and the fear response regulated.

If the body's alarm response occurs more often than required, it means emotions need to be understood and the fear response regulated.

"I feel out of control"

The same is true for losing control, which is also not a consequence or characteristic of panic attacks, although for many people this interpretation feels very real and can be very frightening. As mentioned earlier, interpretations are personal and vary from person to person, but most commonly people describe feeling that they are losing control of their minds and making bad decisions, are losing control of their bodies and may vomit, wet, or soil themselves. It is even possible that someone may feel they could do something dangerous, or harm themselves or others. These interpretations have their own degree of unpleasantness, but panic attacks do not facilitate any of that.

The fight or flight response and consequent
emotions are normal and cause no harm
in the short or long term.

"I am going to die"

Dying from panic attacks has also never happened. The body does not do anything that it cannot tolerate. The fight or flight response and consequent emotions are normal and protective and cause no harm in the short or long term.

Your army of knowledge is getting stronger and more prepared for the battle ahead. You have now understood what panic attacks are, your triggers, the bodily processes involved, and most importantly how you interpret such unpleasant experiences. What is still left to understand is why panic attacks become a problem and how that problem is maintained for so many people. Our journey will now focus on developing that understanding and finding out how your behaviour is the missing piece of the puzzle.

CHAPTER 3

UNPACKING HOW YOU EXPERIENCE PANIC

In this chapter you will try to make sense of your different responses to panic attacks, and learn how the coping mechanisms that you use may actually be making them worse.

What Happens Once You've Had a Panic Attack

Panic is sticky; it sticks to you. Whether you have had a single experience or suffer from recurrent panic attacks, it is likely that you will think about it for a long time after the event. It stays with you not only because it felt bad, but because it was devastating; it broke something inside of you. And because of that, even after it has passed, it is glued onto you, because trying to understand it, forgetting it, or fixing the broken bits will take some time.

So, what happens *after* experiencing one panic attack or, in most cases, several panic attacks?

The most common consequence of having a panic attack is to become fearful of further attacks. If that was not enough, there is also the fear of what the consequences of such episodes might be. You might start having thoughts such as "Will it happen again?", "What is it going to be like?" or "How bad will it be?". These thoughts are unwanted and unpleasant in themselves, but may also lead you to start being vigilant, to try to prevent further panic attacks. This happens because you are either now preoccupied about having another panic attack, or because you are now more aware of your feelings and have become sensitive to them – which makes total sense. The logical way of trying to understand what is going on and whether you will have another panic attack is, of course, to become aware of your body and the physical sensations you feel. For example, you might begin to monitor your heart, whether it is racing or beating faster than usual, because during or after your panic attack you thought you were about to have a heart attack. That is what Alfred (whom I mentioned on page 21) started doing. During his experience on the train he strongly believed he was going to have a heart attack and went to the hospital. Afterwards, he started monitoring his heart and checking his pulse regularly. This goes for a multitude of other physical sensations, like changes in your breathing, trembling, sweating, and others. This monitoring process can become such a priority that you start paying less attention to your normal life, your relationships, goals and pleasures. Even if some things are still somewhat enjoyable, it can feel as if a dark cloud is always above you and a sense of doom starts to be a common part of each day.

As you look for small, physical changes which might suggest another attack, you are constantly vigilant. Unfortunately, such intense vigilance only increases the likelihood of having recurrent panic attacks. Someone once told me that it is like suffering from an excess of inner observation. If you focus inwards and become overly aware of your physical sensations, you will notice them more, will interpret them in certain ways, and have related thoughts. Your thoughts may develop into thinking that you will have a heart attack, and your physical sensations will in turn be exacerbated as your survival response and consequent emotions, such as anxiety, kick in. This then leads to *further* thoughts and interpretations. We have a kind of vicious cycle going on here, represented in the diagram below.

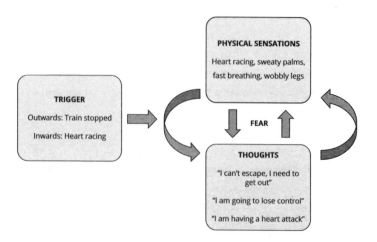

Whether you have experienced just one or several panic attacks, it is logical that you made some interpretations of what you experienced and that you try to protect yourself and prevent future attacks. To do so, however, you start behaving in particular ways.

Protective Behaviours

We are now starting to look at that piece of the puzzle that accounts for what you did during or after your panic attack(s), and what you are potentially doing to try and keep safe and prevent future attacks.

As with the experience of panic, the resulting emotions and interpretations are deeply personal, so it is also expected that protective behaviours vary from person to person. Nonetheless, some are very common, and some characteristics seem to be similar. It is important not only to identify these behaviours, but also to understand if they are actually helping.

Avoidance and escape are the most common protective behaviours. I will start by describing them and then go on to look at more idiosyncratic (i.e. unique for a particular person), yet still frequent, behaviours.

Avoidance

The most common behaviour associated with panic attacks is avoidance. Your life has been shaken up, you are worried or preoccupied, anxious, and feel you cannot endure or cope with further attacks. As a result, you might start to avoid situations in which you experienced such episodes or in which you anticipate having one. For example, Alfred, who had a panic attack on the train, now drives to work.

Avoidance is a logical behaviour. It is also a tricky one because it can become quite addictive. If you start avoiding situations and, as a result, your anxiety reduces (as well as your experience of panic attacks), the likelihood is that your anxiety will generalize and you will start avoiding other situations. If that happens, you might eventually end up with some rather difficult restrictions to your lifestyle. For some people who end up developing severe anxiety disorders, such avoidance might result in being completely housebound, with no opportunity to take part in normal society or to have the rewarding life experiences that are so important for all human beings. It can be devastating.

Avoidance behaviours can be different for everyone, as their personal triggers vary (e.g. some people feel anxious in cinemas, some people feel anxious while having an argument) and include any situation in which a panic attack is anticipated, for example:

- avoiding places such as the cinema, supermarket, certain types of public transport, areas with crowds;
- avoiding situations such as driving, meetings, public presentations, holidays, medical appointments;
- avoiding confrontations, disagreements, and/or arguments with others.
- If you are preoccupied with not having help available when you experience a panic attack, you might start avoiding being on your own.

Some people may also avoid any activity that can cause the physical sensations that they associate with panic. For example:

- If your heart always races during a panic attack, you might start to avoid exercising, walking fast, or doing anything too physical.
- If you are fearful of feeling sick or vomiting, you might start to avoid spicy or fatty foods or reduce your food intake.

The list of avoidance behaviours is endless – it all depends on each person's personal experience of panic attacks. The same goes for those behaviours connected to escape.

Escape

Escaping behaviours are also common and, although not as limiting as full-on avoidance, can be just as detrimental and impairing, even if they also seem to be logical. It makes a lot of sense that, if you experience sensations that you are preoccupied or wary of, you will have the urge to leave whatever situation is causing them. If you are not feeling good and anticipate a panic attack, leaving the situation might reduce such feelings. For this reason, just as with avoidance, escaping behaviours are also rather addictive. The odds are quite high that escaping will work (at least, for the short term) and as a result you will start to use this behaviour more and more often.

Examples of escaping behaviours would be:

- making an excuse to leave a meeting at work because you get a feeling of an impending panic attack;
- excusing yourself to go to the bathroom while out with friends because it is your turn to suggest options for the next holiday together and you anticipate you will have a panic attack if put on the spot;
- travelling by train and disembarking at the next stop rather than at your destination because there is a

long tunnel ahead and you know if the train stops underground you will have a panic attack;
- turning down a good opportunity at work because what it involves makes you preoccupied about panic attacks.

Other Protective Behaviours

People tend to develop and perform a range of different protective behaviours in order to cope, feel safe, or prevent panic attacks. Further to avoidance and escape behaviours these other protective behaviours are adopted by individuals for specific circumstances and are associated with specific thoughts. Therefore, they take different forms depending on the person. They may become something of a routine, so much so that performing them becomes simply a part of one's life. As with avoidance and escape, you might consider these behaviours also logical and helpful, as they seem to either take panic away or keep it at bay, even though they take extra time and remove some of the joy from your life.

Some examples of protective behaviours would be:

- If you are preoccupied about wetting yourself in public and need to go to town, you might plan your route in such detail that you know where all the toilets are.
- If you need to go shopping but anticipate something might happen in the supermarket, you might ask a friend to come with you.

- If you are going out with friends and feel like you might panic, you might choose to have some alcohol beforehand or choose a bar close to your house which you know very well.
- If you are worried about losing control while taking care of your child, you might lock all the knives in the kitchen away.
- If you are feeling out of control in general because of panic attacks, you might feel that controlling what you are able to helps to an extent, and you might find yourself keeping everything organized or putting things in a particular order.
- You might also start carrying what several of my clients have called a "panic kit", which could include items such as water, an energy drink, a paper bag, betablockers, paracetamol, or other items.
- If you are going to speak at a meeting or see a group of people and are preoccupied with sweating and others noticing that you are sweating profusely, you might decide to wear extra layers so it cannot be seen.

Avoidance, escape and other protective behaviours are really varied and depend on how creative you can be in trying to keep yourself safe and the panic at bay.

These behaviours can also be present while you are actually experiencing a panic attack. Imagine you are on a bus and have a panic attack. You might try to manage it by controlling your breathing, taking deep breaths or moving close to the door so you can exit faster than planned. Or you might ask for help, have some water, or ask someone to call an ambulance.

EXERCISE: Identify Your Protective Behaviours

It is now important to identify your own protective behaviours and add that last piece of the puzzle to the information your army of knowledge needs.

Looking back on your panic attacks, think of what you did to either avoid, escape or keep yourself safe in any other ways. Read through the examples in this chapter as a starting point.

Write down as many behaviours as you can identify in your notebook.

You are making great progress, you are becoming an observer of your own experience and so far, you have identified your triggers, physical sensations, your thoughts or interpretations and your behaviour. This is very good. The next step is to understand why these behaviours are indeed the last piece of the puzzle and why they might actually be *maintaining* your panic attacks.

Why These Behaviours are Counterproductive

On the surface, protective behaviours seem very logical. They are put in place because you thought something was about to be dangerous, and they seem to help with enduring and/or keeping you safe. The question is: was there ever any real danger present? Even if you were in a difficult situation (such as giving a public presentation or taking an important exam), was the estimation of danger a reliable one, or was it somehow rather catastrophic? To add to this picture, it is likely that you did not believe that you could cope unless some behaviours were put in place. Overestimating danger while underestimating your ability is the perfect recipe for fear and anxiety.

Overestimating danger while underestimating your ability is the perfect recipe for fear and anxiety.

Why is that?

Well, you might have coped with the panic attack at that point in time, but consequently learned a lesson that is not really true – that if your protective behaviours are *not* put into place, then the worst will happen. This is a hard realization to shift and will inevitably come to rule your life to a certain extent. Being fearful of panic, avoiding it, escaping it, preventing it and enduring it takes priority. To avoid such pain, your life in its purest form is taken away from you. You might also lose confidence in your ability to deal with difficulties, and experience an increase in anxiety itself.

So, are these behaviours helpful *at all*? To answer that question, ask yourself: what is your experience? If you stop the behaviour, does the panic disappear? The answer is probably not. After all, that is why you keep doing them in the first place. This means that while you are trying to fix the symptom, the *cause remains*. In fact, I now challenge you to consider that maybe these behaviours are making the problem worse. Maybe in the short term they are providing some relief and sense of safety, perhaps even some anxiety reduction, but in the long term they are only maintaining or heightening your anxiety.

By engaging in avoidance, escape and other protective behaviours, we miss out on the opportunity to learn to manage panic in a healthy manner.

When someone feels as if they will have a heart attack if they do not leave a particular situation, and they do leave, and no heart attack occurs, what did they learn? They have learned that if they stayed, they would have had a heart attack, and that leaving prevented that outcome. The idea that being in that particular situation is dangerous is now not only very powerful, but also reinforced. By engaging in avoidance, escape and other protective behaviours, we miss out on the opportunity to learn to manage panic in a healthy manner.

If someone with a diagnosed heart condition leaves a situation when they feel as if they are about to have a heart attack, will that prevent the heart attack? The answer is, of course, no. In their case the danger of a heart attack is very real. In cases of panic however, there is no *real* danger present, only the *anticipation* of potential danger.

Breathing Exercises

You may have heard about using breathing control exercises as a means of managing panic attacks. A long time ago such exercises were thought to be useful, but much research has been dedicated to the study of anxiety and it is now known that attempts to control one's breathing during a panic attack actually *contribute* to the maintenance of the problem. This is because breathing control or exercises can also be thought of as protective behaviours. Although research is not conclusive regarding the use of deep breathing to reduce stress and lower cortisol levels, it is known that when used as a protective behaviour, deep breathing is contributing to the knowledge that if you *do not* breathe deeply, something bad will happen. Breathing control can therefore also be a potential problem that maintains and worsens panic attacks over the long term.

Breathing control exercises can actually maintain
and worsen panic attacks over the long term.

In conclusion, because they make panic attacks worse and more frequent over the long term, escape, avoidance and protective behaviours are counterproductive and only serve to heighten fear. We can, then, add another arrow to our drawing, making behaviour part of the vicious cycle.

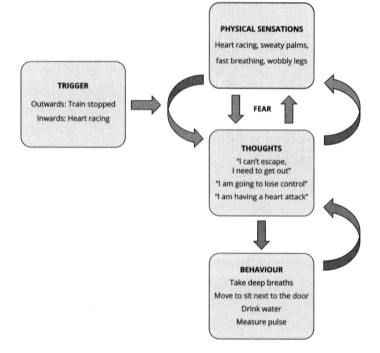

EXERCISE: Identify Your Own Vicious Cycle

To make sense of all the knowledge you have gained so far and put it into perspective with your own experience of panic, think about one or two situations in which you experienced a panic attack.

Use your notebook to draw a cycle for each of those situations, copying the diagram on page 75.

If helpful, refer back to the previous exercises on pages 25, 54 and 71 to help you recall the triggers, physical sensations, interpretations and behaviours you have already identified.

An Alternative Response

Bearing in mind that our protective behaviours (though they might seem perfectly logical) might not be as helpful as we think, what should we *actually* do when panic strikes? This may be difficult to believe, but the answer is: *nothing*.

What should we actually do when panic strikes?
The answer is: *nothing*.

As hard as it is to remember when you are actually having one, panic attacks do not last forever. Our bodies are designed to put processes in place that level out the survival response and, after a time, everything goes back to normal; we do not need to *do* anything about it. The same is true for emotions such as anxiety and fear: they eventually level out.

This physiological response can be represented by a bell-shaped curve (see below). It starts rising with the anticipation of threat, will stay high for a variable amount of time and then will go back down again.

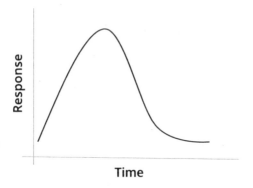

This is because our autonomic nervous system, which controls the physiology of the body in threatening or stressful circumstances, has two components:

- the sympathetic division
- the parasympathetic division

The sympathetic division takes over when we are dealing with threat. It raises our blood pressure, sends blood to our muscles, quickens our breathing, and gets us ready to fight or run. The parasympathetic division, meanwhile, restores homeostasis once the situation is over, or, in other words, it brings everything in our body back to normal when the threat is no longer present.

The bottom line is: if we do not do anything about emotions such as fear and anxiety and let them run their course, everything will go back to normal. Again: panic attacks do not last forever. Research has shown that they can last from just a few minutes to less than an hour.[6] In most cases, they seem to last 4–30 minutes, and, in fact, the more protective behaviours are performed, the longer the attack lasts.

Panic attacks do not last forever.

This is a very important truth, but, needless to say, I am not expecting you to fully believe me at this point. After all, panic feels real, and your army of feelings is still the most powerful force. What I am trying to do here is give your army of knowledge the right weapons to win the war. That will make it a fairer battlefield when we soon come to it. And I am hoping you will at this stage give me the benefit of the doubt and keep reading to find out more.

Reasonable Behaviours

You could also argue that some protective behaviours *are* reasonable and not counterproductive. For example, doing body checks as recommended by doctors for possible health conditions is reasonable. Checking if your front door is locked before going to bed is also reasonable. Reasonable behaviours such as these will not induce panic or anxiety. It's in *overdoing* those behaviours where the trouble lies. So, checking your body above and beyond the recommendations is not a reasonable behaviour. Likewise checking if your front door is closed several times is also unreasonable. I am not suggesting that reasonable behaviours are dropped or changed in any way, but you might want to take another look at the behaviours you consider reasonable and make sure they really are.

Your Progress So Far

Well done! You have just put it all together, identified and learned about your triggers, physical sensations, thoughts and protective behaviours. Looking at your vicious cycles and the notes you have made so far, it is hopefully clear that you are making *permanent* decisions based on *temporary* feelings and emotions, and that needs to change.

I hope that at this point you have a better understanding of your experience of panic, and that it makes sense to you that the physiological response, the emotional response, the thoughts and the behaviours are all interlinked and all influence each other.

We will now look at what you could do differently that may help you better manage your experiences of panic attacks and also reduce their occurrence.

CHAPTER 4

HOW TO RECLAIM YOUR LIFE

We have now given our army of knowledge a massive boost by learning all about panic attacks – their physiology, associated emotions, interpretations and protective behaviours. And because you cannot fight what you do not know, you have also, by completing the exercises in the previous chapters, identified your own unique experience of these. Now it is time to start to fight the war.

I am going to show you how to start using the knowledge you have gained so far to get your life back, to accept your emotions, to develop a healthy relationship with your anxiety, and to reduce (and eventually drop altogether) those behaviours we talked about in Chapter 3. I will continue to guide you through this journey to not only understand but now also change your behaviours in a genuinely helpful way to reclaim your life.

The first step on your journey to accept and develop a healthy relationship with your anxiety is to make your battlefield less frightening by opening up to others about your panic attacks.

Start an Open Dialogue With Family and Friends

Panic attacks can change you and your life in many ways. The experience can be devastating; you might feel utterly bereft. However, because the nature of panic attacks is not altogether easy to understand, you might hide it from those around you. This could be because you believe that most people will not understand what panic attacks are or why you are experiencing them. Or you may worry that people will respond by telling you to "just get over it" and "move on". It might also be the case that talking to others, either family or friends, is nerve-wracking as it is; it might even be one of your triggers.

Isolation is not the best option. Being alone with your fears, preoccupations and anticipation brings on another type of hell.

Whatever the reasoning, isolation is not the best option. By isolation I do not mean being *physically* by yourself, I mean the emotional isolation of not sharing your experiences, feelings, thoughts and needs with anyone else. Being alone with your fears, panic attacks, preoccupations, anticipation and devastation brings on another type of hell. Not only will you have panic attacks, but you are alone in your world, with no support, and at the same time you will need to spend your precious energy pretending everything is okay. When you start to make excuses not to go places, to leave situations, or you start behaving in different ways with and toward others, you become disconnected from your life, potentially from yourself, and also from those around you. It's both devastating and exhausting, and nothing in that picture looks good for mental health.

For this reason, it is a good idea to start opening up
and sharing your experiences with others; with those
you trust.

Communication is a fundamental human tool to ensure
our needs are met – to understand, and to be understood.
When we communicate, we can make sense of ourselves,
the world and whatever topic or issue we are discussing.
This is important when experiencing panic, as such
experience is rarely understood.

Communication is a fundamental human tool
to ensure our needs are met – to understand,
and to be understood.

You are far from alone in suffering from panic attacks, and
after opening up to those who care about you, you might be
surprised by how many people have had similar experiences
or know someone who still does. If at all possible, give it a try
and start talking.

Accept Your Emotions

The next stage in this process is all about starting to change
your experience. To do so, you have to face your feelings,
your emotions and what your fear; there is no other way.
In order to regulate your emotions, you have to experience

them, and to experience them, you have to confront what you fear the most. It might sound like a threatening solution, but there are ways of doing this that can feel less daunting, and I hope you give it a try.

In order to regulate your emotions, you have to experience them, and to experience them, you have to confront what you fear the most.

One of the fundamental steps you have to take is to start accepting your emotions and letting them take their natural course.

When you have a panic attack and you try to control it, or do all that is in your power to avoid reoccurrences, you are *interfering with your emotions.* If you try to control your anxiety using protective behaviours during a panic attack, you interfere with the body's natural ability to go back to normal, and with the process of anxiety levelling out by itself. You are interfering with the natural course of your anxiety and taking away the opportunity for your brain to learn that, in fact, the situation was not dangerous. This is problematic for many reasons, one being that we cannot choose which emotions we avoid and which ones we feel; it is not a selective process. And so, by changing the emotional process, we change the natural course of *all* emotions.

During a panic attack, if you try to control your
anxiety using protective behaviours, you are taking
away the opportunity for your brain to learn that the
situation was not dangerous.

You might think that you are able to numb or supress only
your negative feelings, but you actually end up numbing or
supressing the positive ones, too. Emotions are part of us as
human beings, and pulling away from them or avoiding them
is not going to feel natural or good. You need to befriend
them once again – and not just the positive ones. Although
we tend to see some emotions in a rather negative way, they
all have a function, and anxiety is no different. Anticipating
danger is important, as we discussed earlier; it's overdoing it
that causes problems.

For example, imagine that tomorrow you have a
meeting with the CEO of your company, your manager
and your colleagues. This is something that makes you
feel uneasy; you feel pressured to perform. You need
to present to the whole team what was achieved during
the year and the financial goals for the following year.
Although it is part of your job, you have never done it
before. Whether you have had a panic attack in a meeting
before or not, you feel anxious. You do your best to get
everything ready and make good, informative slides. You
do not have a very restful night's sleep and feel on edge
when you wake up in the morning, but you go to the

meeting. You are sitting at your chair, and when it is your time to present, you stand up. You start your presentation. Your heart starts racing, your breathing becomes faster, you are shaking, you feel sweaty and your mouth is dry. You are having a panic attack. From here, there are two scenarios:

Scenario 1: You keep going. You focus on what is around you, you tell yourself that it is good experience and you will manage, that you know what you are doing. You move to the next slide, you feel shaky and as if your words are not coming as you would like, but you continue on. You try to give examples, look at the audience, ask if they have questions. You see heads nodding, and there is a question. *Oh no! A question!* But you hear it, and you feel your mind racing at 500 miles per hour to formulate an answer. Although it felt for a second like you could not think, the answer was there. You answer the question. You finish your presentation. People say thank you. They recognize is not an easy presentation to put together. Then the team starts brainstorming about the best way to achieve the goals during the following year. You feel exhausted but pleased that you did your job and now know you can do a presentation like this in the future.

Scenario 2: You stop, you focus on your sensations. You don't know why your heart is racing, why you are breathing fast, sweating, and your mouth is dry. You feel awful. You try to move to the next slide, reading the words slowly. You stop, you drink water. Everyone is looking at you. You feel your heart racing even faster, your breathing feels out of control, you are visibly shaking and so sweaty. You put your hand on your chest; it is painful; it feels tight. You look at your manager and say, "I am not okay, I am going to have a heart attack." Everyone stands up, lays you down on the floor, and someone calls an ambulance. Your symptoms continue; you are so scared. The paramedics arrive. They examine you. There is nothing wrong; they say it was anxiety. You feel awful and exhausted. You go home and wonder how in the hell you are going to go back again and do the presentation.

It makes sense to be anxious when you are doing something that you care about but which also makes you feel vulnerable.

In the first scenario, you had a panic attack, you were on edge and anxious. But you let your feelings and emotions run their course. They were there for a while and then they went away. It was exhausting, but nothing bad happened. In fact, research has shown that your feelings of anxiety probably helped your performance, as they kept you alert, sharp, and aware.[7]

It also makes sense to be anxious when you are doing something you care about and is important to you, but which also has a cost and makes you feel vulnerable.

In this scenario, although you did not have previous experience of delivering such a presentation, you wanted to do a good job, and what you were doing was difficult and in front of an audience. Your panic attack was perhaps linked with some previous experiences in which you did not feel good enough or were criticized when things might not have gone well. You then possibly learned that such situations were dangerous. This was an important opportunity to gain new learning, and you did that in scenario one.

Research has shown that feelings of anxiety can help performance, as they keep you alert, sharp and aware.

In the second scenario, you did not let the emotions run their course. You focused inwards, instead of focusing on the presentation, and everything escalated from there. Your prior experiences were the same, but no new learning was gained here. In fact, the idea that such situations are frightening and dangerous has been reinforced.

The only similarity to the first scenario is that nothing bad happened; you did not have a heart attack. Danger was also not present, but you really believed it was, and it was awful. From now on, in the second scenario, you will be expecting to feel bad in similar situations.

How Do You Start Accepting Emotions?

To start accepting the feelings you experience while having a panic attack and letting them run their natural course, it is wise that you start experiencing such emotions gradually.

Start accepting the feelings you experience while having a panic attack and let them run their natural course.

One efficient way of doing this is to start acknowledging what you have learned so far.

First and foremost: anxiety is not dangerous. It is unpleasant, but it is not dangerous. It is a normal emotion and it is trying to tell you something – something about yourself, something that you are uneasy or uncomfortable with. It is also getting you prepared for whatever it foresees to be your response to a threat (imagined or real). Let's try applying that knowledge to your experience of panic attacks in the next exercise.

EXERCISE: Gain a New Perspective

Now that you have a good understanding of your panic attacks and anxiety, revisit the cycles you have drawn for the exercise in chapter 3 (page 76).

Remind yourself of how your physical sensations, emotions, thoughts, and behaviours are related and influence each other.

Now, the challenge in this exercise is to ask yourself to bring *facts* into the picture and bring to light a new perspective.

You can use one or both cycles for the exercise, it is up to you. You may find that practicing with both is helpful. Ask yourself:

1. Why was I anxious?
2. What was my anxiety trying to tell me based on my past experiences?
3. What was the function of the bodily processes involved?
4. What is the new perspective I am bringing to the picture?

Use the table opposite as an example of how to do this exercise.

Questions	Answers
Why was I anxious?	*Because I was standing in a queue in the supermarket and felt trapped.*
What was my anxiety trying to tell me based on my past experiences?	*That I do not like to be trapped because it might be dangerous. I felt that way before, during arguments, or when stuck in traffic. I couldn't get out and thought I was going to lose control. It was awful.*
What was the function of the bodily processes involved?	*To get my muscles ready to escape if I had to.*
What is the new perspective I am bringing to the picture?	*I was not really trapped. I was just queuing. I have been in queues before. There was nothing going on; it was just a false alarm because I don't like the feeling of being trapped.*

This is a really positive step. In this exercise, you practised how to use your army of knowledge, to bring what you know into the picture, and to gain perspective.

From now on, challenge yourself to start using this new perspective in real situations, gradually and at a pace that is empowering, manageable and that you feel comfortable with.

Choose Your Battlefield

It is time to begin an experimenting stage, and to do it successfully, the following steps are key. Keep in mind that recovery *is* possible and reclaiming your life is the goal.

In Chapter 1, you identified your triggers (page 25) and in Chapter 3, what you normally do to keep yourself safe (page 71).

To change these for the better, the first step is to look at the situations you tend to avoid, escape or endure with distress, and find ways to make them less daunting. The table opposite gives you some examples of how you may be able to do this. For example, if you are avoiding situations like going on the train, instead of travelling, you can make it your first step just to go to the platform, which is hopefully less daunting. If you are avoiding specific physical sensations, instead of preventing yourself from experiencing them, it is a good first step to try experiencing them in a more comfortable manner. For example, if you are fearful of your heart beating fast, running on the spot will allow you to feel your heart racing and realize that it is not dangerous or harmful. In the same way, if feeling hot sensations makes you fearful of passing out, dressing with extra layers or turning the heating on allows you to realize how much heat you can actually tolerate and that your fear is unfounded.

You could argue that such examples simply represent more creative ways of keeping you safe. And you would be right. However, these behaviours will help you to start facing your difficulties and practice bringing your army of knowledge to the front of the battlefield. Progressively you will reduce these strategies and get closer to experiencing the feared situations with no protective behaviours at all.

Trigger	Making them less daunting
Situations and places	
Train travel	Go to the platform only Travel only one stop or for a short period of time Go to a well-known location Go with someone you trust Go out outside of rush hour
Crowded places	Go there when not too crowded but with some people Go with someone you trust
Queues	Choose to queue in a small queue Go with someone you trust
Being alone	Ask the person you are normally with to start leaving for short periods of time Start going out alone for short periods of time
Driving	Short distances Well-known roads Go with someone you trust
Running	Short distances Pace yourself Go with someone you trust
Physical sensations	
Heart racing	Run on the spot
Dizziness	Spin around
Sweating	Put on several layers and turn the heating on

EXERCISE: Make Your Triggers Less Daunting

Earlier on, during chapter 1 (page 25) you identified your triggers. Find the exercise in your notebook to remind yourself what those were.

It is time to start fighting your feelings with your army of knowledge.

To do so, consider and write down potential ways to make approaching the battlefield less daunting, using the table on page 95 as a guide.

After creating your own table, you will have a plan. You have developed a strategy to approach your battlefield in a less intimidating way.

You are ready to start fighting your feelings in a gradual manner and gain real evidence about how your body works, how your interpretation of events is not accurate and how your protective behaviours are counterproductive.

I will help you step onto your chosen battlefield in the next few pages.

Go to War

When you start feeling any physical sensations, tell yourself what you know. Remind yourself of what you learned from reading the section of this chapter on accepting your emotions (page 85). Stay in the situation, do what you planned to do to make it less frightening (from the exercise opposite), and find out what happens.

Using Mantras

Many people I have worked with over the years like to use mantras (phrases they repeat to themselves) to keep fighting alongside their army of knowledge. Here are some examples:

- "It is just anxiety"
- "Anxiety is not dangerous"
- "I can trust myself"
- "My body is ready and knows what it's doing"
- "I don't need to make anything out of this, it is not worth my interpretation"
- "It is normal, it is just an emotion"
- "It is all in my head, all is normal"

EXERCISE: Come Up With Your Own Mantra

If you find mantras useful, use the knowledge that you have gained so far to come up with your own, or choose one or more from the list on page 97.

Either way, use your notebook to make a note of your chosen mantra(s).

If it works for you, stick them around the house in places you are likely to see them throughout the day.

Whether you choose to use mantras or not, it is important that, while using your army of knowledge, you stay in the situation, bring to your mind all the information you have learned so far and, instead of using your usual protective behaviours, do what you planned to do in the exercise on page 96 to make your battlefield less daunting.

In the next exercise, we will look at the steps you can take to achieve this.

EXERCISE: Experiment With Your Triggers

Choose a trigger from the exercise on page 25 to start experimenting with. After making your choice, it is time to put your army of knowledge to the test.

Go to your battlefield, implement your strategies from page 96 to make it slightly less daunting, and face it. It is time for the first fight between your army of knowledge and your army of feelings to take place.

Instead of reacting with your protective behaviours:

- Ask yourself if the situation is actually dangerous.
- Look around you and remind yourself where you actually are.
- Try to not focus on your feelings or physical sensations, no matter how unpleasant they might feel, as they are not dangerous.
- Focus on what you are doing and your environment; observe others around you.
- Think about whether the feelings you are having matches the current situation or might be related to something else.
- Let the emotions run their natural course and level out.
- If you feel the urge to make it better or keep yourself safe in any way, do not; tell yourself you know that you do not need to do anything.

- Trust yourself and what you *know*, no matter how you *feel*.
- Give yourself the opportunity to realize all of that while experiencing anxiety.

After the event has passed, write down your new experience and the new evidence that you gathered.

Start by writing down what your chosen trigger was and which protective behaviour you used to perform in the past to keep yourself safe.

Then write down your new strategy to make your battlefield less daunting; your new plan. Also write down what you thought would happen by adopting this strategy; what did you anticipate would happen?

After that, write down what actually happened, what you noticed was happening in your body and how you felt during and after this first fight.

To finish, I suggest you start building up new evidence and new knowledge. Reflect and write down what you have learned. What evidence do you now have that you do not need to use protective behaviours and that your fears do not come true?

Use the table opposite as an example.

Trigger	*Heart racing*
Past protective behaviour	*Never rush or run, control my breathing, sit down*
My new strategy	*Run on the spot for 30 seconds and do not control my breathing and do not sit down. Let my body recover naturally and do not focus on the symptoms.*
What I thought would happen	*My heart would race really fast, I would have a panic attack and a heart attack*
What actually happened	*My heart was racing fast, I was breathing fast, I felt out of control but did not try to control anything. When I stopped, I allowed my breathing to catch up, my heart gradually went back to normal and I was fine.*
What I have learned	*That my heart accelerates when I run, my breathing also gets faster, but also that it all goes back to normal without doing anything about it. I do not need to sit down or control my breathing or focus on myself*

Now, experiment with a different trigger and again record the outcome. Do the same for the other triggers you have identified in the exercise on page 25. It might feel difficult or exhausting to try to achieve and gain evidence in a short period of time.

So, I recommend that you try new strategies for triggers on different days or every few days. It is important that you do it at your own pace, allowing yourself time to learn and to take in all this new important information.

Experimenting with your triggers might not be easy, but it is also empowering as your start discovering what you are actually able to do and what your strengths are. I hope you are kind to yourself and feel proud of your achievements and determination to reclaim your life one step at a time. Despite how hard it can be, you are learning and facing your fears.

If you found this exercise difficult, and perhaps used some old habits such as your usual protective behaviours, do not feel disheartened. Go back to the exercise where you made your triggers less daunting (page 96) and think about ways to make it more gradual, to break it down further. For example, make the challenge shorter in duration (e.g. run on the spot for 15 seconds; stay on the train platform only for a few minutes or just go to the entrance of the station, etc.). Then try to experiment with your triggers again. After all, you are learning; learning about yourself, your feelings and emotions and learning what you can do to change them. There is nothing to lose, only something to gain, and you are not alone.

If you found the exercise hard, remember
you are learning; learning about yourself, your feelings
and emotions and learning what you can
do to change them.

If you managed to complete a few experiments, do not
stop there. After the first few attempts, it is important
to keep going, to keep fighting your war. To do so, you
need to experiment more, and try the next harder thing.
Increase the difficulty level and gradually remove the
behaviours that were making the previous experiments
more manageable and tolerable. Keep walking. As
Churchill once said, "If you are going through hell,
keep going."

The Aim is to Accept Not Avoid

Try to remember that the aim of the experiments
is not to try to *avoid* having panic attacks or anxiety.
Instead, a successful experiment means you
experience high levels of anxiety or even a panic
attack, but you do nothing about it. That means
you are doing well. You are not resorting to your
protective behaviours which are counterproductive
(see page 71).

Eventually, as you face your triggers and accept your feelings and emotions, your anxiety will reduce and you will not have such intense experiences anymore. That will happen as a result of what you have learned during your experiements: the evidence you have gathered shows you that what you thought was going to happen does not, in fact, actually happen. All of this is likely to happen as you reduce the number of counterproductive protective behaviours you use.

Reflect On and Develop Your Experiments

While moving from one set of experiments to more challenging ones, it might be good to ask yourself:

- What am I still scared about?
- What am I still not convinced of?

The answers to these questions can then be used to design new experiments.

For example, if instead of avoiding running (because of experiencing heart palpitations and the fear of having a heart attack) you are now running accompanied and at a moderate pace (which is in itself a great achievement), your army of feelings is actually still winning, as you still believe that if you ran faster or by yourself you would have a heart attack. In the same way, you might still believe that if you stayed for longer in the shop while feeling dizzy and hot, you would have fainted. This is important and these questions give you clues and hints about what still needs attention and what you can do next.

Please keep in mind that even if scenarios are
frightening, you can challenge them
in a gradual manner.

So, in these scenarios, for the next experiments, it would be important to run faster, to be alone, and to stay in the shop for longer. Please keep in mind that even if these scenarios are still frightening, you can challenge them in a gradual manner.

The table on page 106 gives some examples of how to make the experiments more challenging based on the previous situations we have covered.

Trigger	Making them less daunting
Situations and places	
Train travel	Travel for a period of time Go to a new location Go alone Go during rush hour
Crowded places	Go there when more crowded Go in alone with someone waiting outside Go alone
Queues	Choose the queue randomly Go in with someone waiting outside
Being alone	Ask the person you are normally with to start leaving for longer periods of time Start going out for longer periods of time
Driving	Longer distances Random roads Go alone
Running	Longer distances Faster pace Go alone
Physical sensations	Start engaging in normal life activities and start dropping any protective behaviours you identify

**EXERCISE: Plan Your Next Sequence
of Experiments**

Following the example in the table opposite, use your
notebook to write down your next steps to make the
battlefield less daunting (similar to what you did in
the exercise on page 99) and plan your next sequence
of experiments.

Then, continue fighting.

Face your fears one experiment at a time, and
after each one, spend some time recording it in
your notebook, reflecting on your learning, and
accumulating the evidence that supports your army
of knowledge.

Gaining Ground on the Battlefield

What you have done so far deserves praise, and I hope you
are congratulating yourself as your army of knowledge is
gaining ground on the battlefield. Taking care of yourself
and acknowledging your achievements and strengths is
important (as I will talk about further in chapter 5).

It is time to aim to remove *all* behaviours (previous
protective behaviours *and* the new behaviours used to make
the battlefield less daunting), as you have now accumulated

enough learning and evidence that you can do this; evidence that experiencing anxiety is not dangerous and your fears are not true. To do that, your new experiments should be carried out without *any* protective behaviours or strategies. See the examples opposite.

You have now accumulated evidence to show that experiencing anxiety is not dangerous and your fears are not true.

At this stage, you no longer need to plan frequent experiments, as long as you are living your life as you were before experiencing panic attacks, or as you would like to right now.

If you do not feel ready for this next stage, go back and focus on the exercises on pages 99 and 107. Keep experimenting with your triggers and reducing your protective behaviours until you feel you have built up enough evidence to proceed.

Trigger	Making them less daunting
Situations and places	
Train travel	Travel spontaneously Go alone Go out wherever you want or have to go
Crowded places	Go to crowded places Go alone Go to random places, crowded or not
Queues	Choose to queue randomly Go alone
Being alone	Stay alone for long periods of time Go out alone and stay for as long as you need or want
Driving	Go wherever you have to go Go alone or accompanied
Running	At whatever pace Whatever location Go alone or accompanied
Physical sensations	Continue engaging in normal life activities, drop any remaining protective behaviours, and focus on your environment and whatever task you have at hand.

What About Anticipation?

Before we move on, it is important to talk about anticipation and its associated feelings. We spoke about anticipation when learning about triggers in chapter one (page 21). For some people, anticipation is, in itself, a big drive for avoidance, escape and protective behaviours. It is possible to manage the emotions anticipation brings on for you, as well as the emotions you have in certain situations or places. You might have panic attacks because you are anticipating either doing one of the tasks you set yourself to do, or because of something that is about to happen in the future, like having a surgical procedure, going to the dentist, failing an exam or a driving test, for example. Imagining that something can go wrong can be just as unpleasant as the reality, and can trigger the same or very similar physiological responses as being in the real situation. Therefore, it is important not to engage in such scenarios. Remember: these thoughts are assumptions, not facts. And you now have a great amount of evidence that your fears are not true.

Remember: anticipatory thoughts
are assumptions, not facts.

To an extent, it is of course important to anticipate what comes next in our lives, and normally the plans we make for ourselves are clear. The path to get there, however, is often ambiguous and less clear. Instead of focusing on what we would like for our future, let's instead focus on the steps we need to take to get there. You do not want to control your life or your future; you want to engage with your life right now, every step of the way.

You do not want to control your life or your future;
you want to engage with your life right now,
every step of the way.

Using what this book wants to achieve as an example, your ultimate goal would be to accept your feelings and emotions and reclaim your life. So, instead of focusing on that goal, let's focus on each and every step you need to take to get there; one at a time. So, if, when you have decided what experiment you are going to do, your mind gets overwhelmed with anticipatory thoughts such as "What if I feel bad on the train?", or "What if something goes wrong while I do the experiment?", you can remind yourself that you are not doing that experiment right now, and that you will deal with it, if it ever happens, at *that* point in time. Remind yourself that you now have the knowledge to fight, and that you trust yourself to use this knowledge to the best of your ability. Now, you choose to focus on "right now" in your life, on what is meaningful to you.

The same is true for anticipating other situations mentioned: having a surgical procedure, going to the dentist, failing an exam or a driving test. Stay in the "here and now". You are not going through that situation at this present moment in time, and indulging in such scenarios takes you away from your life. Trying to control what comes next only makes you feel out of control *right now*. It is not dangerous in this present moment, you cannot fight or resolve anything, but because you are living your future before it even happens, you feel helpless and scared. Engage with life and do what you *can* do.

Trying to control what comes next only makes
you feel out of control *right now*.

The Protective Behavior of Procrastination

A common protective behaviour related to anticipation is procrastination, which we all know so well. Living in a scary future freezes you, and you stop doing what is meaningful and important in the present. So, once again, stay in the now, do what you *can* do – see your friends, go to the gym, study a chapter for the exam; start doing things. Get into action.

If you are a perfectionist and find doing something daunting because it will not be good enough, do not procrastinate. Start doing it *badly*, forget the outcome and improve as you go along. You will soon find out it might not be as bad as you thought. This is how you will start to feel in control again. And when the day comes, go for it: trust yourself and others. Let the emotions run their natural course. Give your brain a chance to learn differently.

Trust yourself. Let emotions run
their natural course.

Addressing Anticipation

To make sure you address all your triggers, let's think about how you can fight on the last bit of ground left on your battlefield. Let's think of gradual ways to use your army of knowledge to deal with anticipatory-related triggers, if any. The tables on pages 114–115 show the actions you can take to minimize anticipatory protective behaviours.

Anticipation	Protective behaviour	What to do instead
What if I have an illness that the doctors cannot find?	Check the body frequently, multiple times Google symptoms Seek reassurance from my partner	Gradually reduce checking Do not google symptoms Gradually reduce reassurance seeking Trust yourself to notice when something is actually wrong Trust medical guidelines Tell yourself you are fine now and you will focus on a problem whenever you actually have one Focus on your life and what you have to do instead

Anticipation	Protective behaviour	What to do instead
What if something goes wrong during my presentation?	Over plan	Only plan as you would if you were not anxious; what is reasonable
	Rehearse many times the night before instead of sleeping	
		Rehearse only a couple of times
	Check slides over and over	Check slides once
	Decide to not allow any questions from the audience	Allow questions
		Trust yourself to deal with whatever happens
		Acknowledge that you know what you are talking about and you will do the best you can
		Sleep so you are rested for the presentation the day after

EXERCISE: Make a Plan of Action

It's time to develop a strategy to drop any protective behaviours that you use to deal with anticipatory anxiety and panic. (If at this stage anticipation is no longer one of your triggers, please move on to the next section of the book.)

In the tables on pages 114–115 you have examples of how to gradually experiment with your protective behaviours by dropping one at time.

In your notebook, make a table for each of the anticipation factors and protective behaviours that you are aware of. Add ideas on how to challenge and change these behaviours.

It is now time to give it a try. Next time you feel yourself anticipating a panic attack, try the alternative activities.

As before, use your army of knowledge in the battle and remind yourself of the evidence you have gathered so far. Stick to your plan.

After each experiment write in your notebook what you have learned.

Signing the Peace Treaty

If the principles and suggestions outlined here have
worked for you so far, then your army of knowledge has
won against your army of feelings. Your emotions ran their
natural course and you have learned about yourself and
your emotions, which is empowering. You have done the
hardest part, but now there is no longer any need to keep
fighting. It is now time to sign a peace treaty. It is time for
your knowledge to live alongside your feelings; it is time for
co-operation and friendship. You not only need to win the
war, but win the peace.

It is time for your knowledge to live alongside
your feelings; it is time for co-operation
and friendship.

To achieve and maintain friendship between your armies,
it is important to keep living your life as normal, to go out
and do everything you want to do. If your emotions take
over somewhat, that is not a problem or a setback of any
kind. In fact, it is actually quite normal. It can take a while
for your brain to fully register the new information you
have been – and are still – collecting. That information
will be part of your memory some day and will impact on

how your emotions manifest. But, as I say, that takes time. You see, it is easy to create new memories; it's harder to record them in your mind for good.

If your emotions take over, that is not a setback
of any kind. It can take a while for your brain
to fully register the new information
you are collecting.

It is also important, when living your life as normal, to create diversity in your day-to-day actions. If you find yourself making the exact same train journey, sitting in the same chair in meetings, planning things in the same way, eating similar foods, etc., you might find that these start to unconsciously become protective behaviours. So, try to vary things; be spontaneous and find out how much you can do, how much you can cope with, and enjoy dealing with whatever life puts in your way.

EXERCISE: Summary and Continuous Application of Learning

To acknowledge your strengths and your extraordinary ability to face whatever difficulties life might bring upon you, it is useful to summarize what really worked for you, what you learned, the evidence you collected, and how you are going to use this learning in your life from now on.

In your notebook, answer the following questions:

- What really did work for me?
- What did I learn from doing the experiments?
- What is the most important evidence that I collected?
- What are my strengths?
- How am I going to use this learning in my life from now on?

Refer back to this summary whenever you are feeling like you need encouragement – you have already come so far.

Notice Your Progress

No matter what happens next, I hope you are proud of yourself. None of this is easy to consider, let alone do. I have been literally asking you to face your biggest fears, but I do so because I know that this knowledge- and evidence-based approach *works*, as I've seen time and time again in my clients. Here is some feedback I have heard from clients over the years about the approach I describe in this book:

> *"It was absolutely amazing (literally). Completely changed my life from not wanting to live to now being on one of the highs of life and in control of myself as opposed to being controlled by my thoughts."*

> *"This therapy was very surprising and informative. It worked better than I ever expected it to. It has changed my life for the better and I would recommend it to anyone."*

> *"This is a therapy process from which you will get out as much you put in. I've tried various different therapies in the past, and have never before felt so invested in my recovery. I would recommend it to anyone."*

> *"Working with this approach made a profound positive impact in my life. The problem I sought help with was quickly and sustainably resolved, and far beyond. It helped me to discover and implement strategies that I have put to work in many other areas*

*of my life too. I now feel more able to realise my
potential and work effectively at whatever I am doing,
and also more able to enjoy and take pride in myself
and my work."*

I really mean it when I say I *know* that you can reclaim your
life and change it for the better, that you can learn to trust
yourself. Trying to control everything in our lives does
not help us as human beings. The world is uncertain, and
learning to tolerate uncertainty and trust in your ability to
cope, rather than underestimating it – no matter how scary
the world might seem – is your best weapon.

The less you try to control anything, the more in control
you will feel. We are, as human beings, equipped to deal with
whatever is ahead on our path.

Tolerating uncertainty and trusting in your ability
to cope, no matter how scary the world might
seem, is your best weapon.

Signs You Might Need Additional Help

If, after working through the steps outlined in this book so
far, you are either still very anxious or still experience panic
attacks, do not despair. This is not a failure on your part.
It is fantastic that you read this book and tried the process

described here; it shows that you are motivated to change your life and circumstances.

Remember, you are not alone. Some people are more anxious than others and, for several different reasons (genetics and other biological factors, various psychological factors, and past learned experiences), it is harder to recover for some than for others. The good news is that you still have options available to you. As we have discovered, panic is *very* sticky, but the brain can adapt, can learn, and it *is* possible to change. Your future does not have to be ruled by anxiety and panic attacks.

Panic is *very* sticky, but the brain can adapt, can learn, and it *is* possible to change. Your future does not have to be ruled by anxiety and panic attacks.

One option is to work alongside someone that can guide you every step of the way toward recovery, which many people find very helpful. The right person for that is an experienced cognitive behavioural therapist or clinical psychologist. They will try to understand your difficulties and potentially identify why trying to recover by yourself was not successful. At the end of this book, you will find several resources which will help you find the best person to work with toward reclaiming your life.

Joining groups that aim to support those that experience panic attacks is another route you could take. These are often run by individuals that have had similar experiences themselves, or sometimes by a therapist. You will have the opportunity to share your experience and also hear from others. They will also work with you toward recovery.

Some people prefer the help of medication. There is medication that can help reduce your symptoms and improve your quality of life, so speaking to your doctor about it and discussing options is the first step. A combination of therapy and medication is yet another route you could choose.

No matter what your preference, I would suggest you speak to your doctor if you are still struggling with panic. They will advise on these options and guide you on the steps to take next.

CHAPTER 5

SELF-CARE AND PANIC ATTACKS

What is Self-Care?

So far in this book, we have talked about things that are out of your control, and we have discovered that there are things that you do to *try* to be in control that actually contribute to you feeling *out* of control. It is, then, a nice and potentially refreshing change to talk about some choices you can make that you *are* in control of, with the additional benefit of contributing to your health and wellbeing.

What I am talking about is self-care.

Although a popular topic these days, self-care is far from a new concept. Broadly, the idea is that you focus on improving how you feel in your body and mind by making good choices in your everyday life.

Self-care is a deliberate way of living where you actively choose the best options from the things under your control in order to take care of yourself.

Self-care is a deliberate way of living where you actively choose the best options from the things under your control in order to take care of yourself. It is all about taking the time you need to take care of yourself, whether you are currently healthy or not. Self-care is what you do to maintain your health, to prevent illness, or to manage an illness if you are unwell.

Buying and reading this book leads me to assume that you have experienced or are currently experience panic attacks, and therefore, self-care should be important to you. You need to take the time to take care of yourself.

To be able to do this, it is important that you first *know yourself*. Who are you? What makes you happy? What makes you unhappy? How much can you take on and do? What are your limits? When should you stop and rest?

To take care of yourself, it is important
that you first *know yourself*.

EXERCISE: Identify Your Needs

There is no such thing as the right time to start self-care. Why not start right now?

Start reflecting on how you can start taking care of yourself – or improve how you do it if you already make time for yourself in your life.

Ask yourself the following questions and write down the answers in your notebook.

- Who am I?
- What makes me happy and what does not?
- What are my needs? Which of these are not met?
- How much can I take on?
- What are my limitations?
- When should I stop and rest?
- How much time do I spend doing something for myself?

Some of these questions may have been hard for you to answer, and that's ok.

We'll look further into your answers in the next exercise and explore what self-care might look like for you.

Self-care is Something You Can Control

As a human being, you have needs. These needs vary from person to person but, generally, we require shelter, food, rest, sleep, to do pleasurable things, exercise, to be cared for and care for ourselves, among others (which might include cultural beliefs and practices, spirituality, etc.).

It sounds great, doesn't it? That's because it *is*. It is great because it is *under your control*. You can do as much as possible to manage your own wellbeing, to be as healthy as possible, and that is empowering. You can feel confident and be informed about taking care of yourself and depend less often on your doctor and your country's health system. That means that, with the choices you make for yourself, to an extent you can control your own health and prevent being unwell in the long run.

Why is Self-Care Important?

The world is a busy place these days, and our lives are often fast-paced and stressful. For many people, their own needs are perhaps only rarely a priority. There are so many responsibilities and *other* people to take care of, that It's easy to forget yourself. You may even think that putting your needs above those of others is a bit selfish. To live a healthy and potentially happy life, however, self-care is a key piece of the puzzle.

You may think that putting your needs above
those of others is selfish; however, to live a healthy
and happy life, self-care is key.

Life is often overwhelming – add to that the fact you
experience panic attacks. As if time was already not of the
essence, you have even less time to focus on yourself and
on your life. You are anxious and feel limited by your fears;
everything is harder. Even if you now think or focus on
yourself more, that does not happen in the best of ways or
for the best of reasons. You focus on yourself because you
are scared. To help you reclaim your life, self-care becomes
really important.

You might be thinking that, yes, this all sounds great,
but you do not have the privilege of sparing some time for
yourself, or cannot afford to do so. How can you possibly fit
anything else into your full-on daily schedule of family, work,
errands, commitments, housework, etc.? Time for self-care? Is
that a joke? Well, actually, it's not.

Here are some of the reasons why it is important to give
self-care a try.

You End the Vicious Cycle

The lack of time for caring for oneself can have
consequences that also work as a vicious cycle, similar
to what we looked at before with panic attacks. By not

taking care of yourself, you start having less energy, less motivation, difficulties concentrating, irritability, less patience, headaches, stress, anxiety, etc. When you feel like this, the burden feels heavier and you try harder. As a result, it feels more and more like you do not have time for yourself. This becomes a self-fulfilling prophecy, and all because you are trying your best.

The Benefits Outweigh the Costs

Self-care does not have to take that much time and/or cost you financially, and if you feel good you are better able to take care of others, so prioritizing yourself is not selfish at all, and the benefits are priceless. It can improve your mental health, your physical health; it can reduce your stress and anxiety; it can help you to establish better relationships and increase your self-esteem. All with choices *you can make yourself*.

Fitting Self-Care Into Your Day

If the idea of carving out time for self-care seems impossible, try instead to focus on what you *can* do and less on what you cannot – to start with what *is* possible and then increase as time goes by. Here are some ideas on how to make self-care a part of your life even if you have a busy schedule.

Activities	Make it possible
Spend quality time with loved ones	Cook a meal for two days: spend one day playing with the kids or watching some TV with a partner instead of cooking.
Do something you enjoy	Read for 10 minutes on the train; cook while watching something you like on TV; put music on while in the shower or cooking. Twice a week play a musical instrument, knit, draw or engage with any other hobby for 15 minutes instead of doing one of your usual household chores.
Relaxing activities	Have a bath once a week; delegate dinner to your partner; sit and watch a series you like for half an hour; have a date night.
Laugh	Watch comedy; call a friend and talk about good things; play silly games with kids.
Eat healthy foods	Switch a comforting, unhealthy item for an healthy, tasty one.
Exercise	Go for a walk on your lunch break; get off the bus a few stops before your destination and walk for a while; dance while cooking or cleaning.

Activities	Make it possible
Attend recommended health check-ups	Go to the health check-ups recommended by your doctor (it will only take up more of your time if you get unwell).
Rest	Stop for 5 minutes for a cup of tea; have a 10-minute break every 2 hours or so.
Sleep	Try to sleep for 7 hours per day – treat yourself on weekends.
Reduce activities you do not like	Check the news less or only once a day; create designated cleaning times rather than doing it bit by bit; unfollow or snooze people on social media.
Reduce alcohol intake	Do not exceed recommended units per week.
Stop smoking	Ask for support or consider stopping by yourself.
Avoid drugs	Ask for support or stop yourself.

EXERCISE: Am I Taking Care of Myself?
How Can I Make it Possible?

No matter how impossible it might seem, it is clear
that there are so many benefits to self-care, that giving
it a try is important. Because you also experience
or have experienced panic attacks, taking time for
yourself, reclaiming your life and having your needs
met is a no-brainer. Let's consider the best way to
make this happen.

Ask yourself, and reflect in your notebook: Am I taking
care of myself? Then start your self-care journey by
giving an honest answer, without judgement or
criticism. Just say it as it is, no *ifs* and no *buts*. Write it
down.

Leave it there for a little while. Let's implement some
more self-care by grabbing a cup of tea or your
favourite drink. Why not top it up with a biscuit? Now
you are ready.

Look at your honest answer again. Now ask yourself:
How can I do better? How can I make taking care of
myself a possibility?

Use the following strategy to find as many solutions as
possible:

Write down all the things, big or small, you would like to do to take care of yourself, to feel better. Remind yourself of the list you made of your needs and the things that make you happy in the previous exercise (page 129).

Break them down as much as possible. For example, instead of reading your favourite book, break it down into reading 10 minutes of your favourite book.

Think of your day and consider how you can find a spare 10 minutes, or how you can squeeze two tasks into one to gain a bit of extra time, or how you could combine a task with something you like (e.g. having a shower with music in the background, reading a book while having lunch, or going for a walk while calling a friend).

Grab your diary (if you do not have one, think about your weekly routine). Where could you spare 10 minutes? What activities could you combine?

Choose a couple of the activities you wrote down, and put them in your diary. Stick to it!

Although self-care is mostly about you, it does not exclude being supported by a doctor. In fact, self-care is also about knowing and understanding when to ask for help and support. It is all about making your own choices at the right time.

Unhealthy Behaviours To Be Aware Of

Some behaviours are known to be detrimental to your general health and can increase the odds of experiencing panic attacks. These are some examples of how a lack of self-care, either by lack of knowledge, choice, or circumstances, can lead to anxiety and panic.

- **Lack of sleep**. Unhealthy sleep patterns have been associated with poor mental health, and sleep deprivation can cause anxiety and panic.
- **Stress**. Having a stressful lifestyle and experiencing stress for long periods of time can increase anxiety and the chance of having panic attacks.
- **Smoking**. Smoking can affect not only your physical health but also your mental health. Although generally smokers report that having a cigarette is relaxing, smokers are three to four times more likely to experience panic attacks and the risk reduces if the person stops smoking.
- **Alcohol**. Alcohol can relax you temporarily, but in the long term it can actually cause crippling anxiety and panic attacks, as it alters the brain processes related to the fight or flight response. Further to that, it also increases concerns about what you did while under the influence.
- **Drugs**. Using drugs can also be linked to anxiety and panic attacks. For example, cannabis can lead to symptoms remarkably similar to those of a panic attack.

If someone is already an anxious person or has had panic attacks in the past, the use of cannabis can be a trigger for such experiences. Withdrawal from other stimulant drugs (amphetamines, caffeine, MDMA, cocaine, etc.) also have anxiety and panic attacks as side effects.

Why Suffering From Panic Attacks Can Make Self-Care Hard

As we've discussed, panic changes you, and it can be devastating. It is also sticky, and stays with you for a while; it changes your life and what you see ahead of you. Making yourself a priority is no longer an option (if it has ever been); now the priority is to avoid further panic attacks and their consequences. This will inevitably make self-care harder.

Panic is limiting, and it also limits the ability
to prioritize self-care.

For some people with anxiety and panic attacks, the idea of self-care can be a trigger in itself. It can feel like a pressure, as "something else to do", which in a lot of cases is not possible. This can create feelings of guilt, so, although self-care is important, it is not always helpful when one experiences panic attacks.

It is not all that surprising that, for someone who experiences panic attacks, the idea of exercising, relaxing, or doing pleasant activities (like going to the cinema, socialising, relaxing alone, etc.) might not be the most appealing, especially if panic attacks are generally experienced in such situations. Panic is limiting, and it also limits the ability to prioritize self-care.

The experience of panic attacks also makes self-care difficult in other ways. People with panic attacks often find that alcohol takes the anxiety away; they feel that they can relax for a while if they drink. The same goes for smoking and the use of other drugs. As explained on pages 137–138, however, these substances can then increase the experience of both anxiety and panic. In turn, people will drink, smoke and take drugs more often. It is another kind of vicious cycle that can be difficult to break.

If you feel you may have an over-reliance on alcohol or drugs, it is important to work on your recovery first, and introduce self-care choices as you go along, when it feels possible. The combination of the two will aid your recovery, help to sign the peace treaty between feeling and knowledge and become a person that loves yourself. You will also become in tune with your emotions and needs.

As you progress and start to feel empowered, as you begin to recognize that your knowledge and feelings are becoming friends, please accept that self-care is one of the most important things you can do to keep the peace between your armies of knowledge and feelings. Self-care can help you maintain your achievements, and promote your future wellbeing.

CONCLUSION

RECLAIMING YOUR LIFE IS POSSIBLE

The Importance of Acceptance

However bad you might be feeling about your panic attacks, know that *you do not have to feel this way*. Recovery is possible, and acceptance is key.

Accepting that you have a problem is a really important step to changing your life, and reading this book is a sign of such acceptance. Actively looking for answers and helpful strategies to cope is the way to go, otherwise you might find you are fighting this war with the wrong weapons.

Recovery is possible, and acceptance is key.

As we explored in Chapter 2, *anxiety is a normal emotion*. It may feel stressful, but it is there for a reason, and you do not want it to go away completely. Instead, you need to co-exist with it, walk with it hand in hand. As hard as it may be to believe, a certain amount of anxiety will help you perform at a higher level, make better decisions, and perhaps even survive dangerous situations. Accept it as a friend.

A certain amount of anxiety will help you make better
decisions, and survive dangerous situations.
Accept it as a friend.

When anxiety is all over the place, takes over your life
and leads to panic attacks, it is not helpful anymore, and
you cannot function. Accept that *this is a problem that
has a solution*. Stop knocking your head against a wall by
looking for more protective behaviours and accept that
the best way to move on is to try something different – to
change your strategy. Otherwise, at the end of the day, it is
your head that will break, not the wall. The steps detailed
throughout this book are the most effective ways I have
found to change the strategy.

The Benefits of Panic Attacks

I am going to dare to say that there are actually benefits
to experiencing panic attacks. Several of my clients
have said that, even though they would never have
chosen to have a panic attack, that it was painful,
frightening and sometimes brutal, they are now glad of
the experience because it has allowed them to learn so
much about themselves.

Experiencing panic attacks, understanding them
and overcoming them can be empowering. You
learn about your emotions, what they are, their
function, and how to allow them to just *be there*, to

experience them naturally and in a healthy manner. You will find you no longer try to suppress or hide from them.

As a result of experiencing panic attacks, you also learn that your anxiety is more of a friend than you previously believed. It helps you, protects you, and keeps you sharp and ready. That is good to know. As a result, you discover that you can cope with the world and what it has to offer much better than you thought. That is also empowering; you no longer underestimate your ability to cope.

This is an opportunity to learn about your emotions, and how to allow them to just *be there*, to experience them naturally and in a healthy manner.

As you are now more at peace and trust yourself more, so your relationships might improve, becoming less focused on keeping yourself safe and/or trying to be someone you are not.

As if these were not enough rewarding and meaningful benefits, you have also learned that *there are no limits to what you can do*. You can face your fears. You can stand up after you have fallen and, more importantly, you know you can fight the hardest of wars. To me, these sound like pretty incredible benefits to come from such a difficult experience.

Final Thoughts

I would like to finish with some suggestions that might help you to not only face your fears but also to have a more rewarding and healthy relationship with yourself and with your life.

- **Accept yourself**. Be who you are, trust yourself to fight whatever is ahead. You can do it because you are better than you think at resolving real difficulties; it is the *less* real ones that are the problem.
- **Focus on one day at a time**, one problem at a time, and give yourself a chance. This is a great opportunity to see what you can do and what you are made of.
- **Embrace your emotions**. It is as important to be sad as it is to be happy. All emotions are healthy, so do not avoid them; learn from them, grow with them.
- **Do not aim for perfection**; it does not exist. Aim to do the best you can under the circumstances. Accept it is all you can do and that it is as close to perfection as you can get.
- **Do not procrastinate**. Start doing small things, badly if necessary, and then make them better. Nothing will make you feel more in control than putting things into action. Be an active participant in your life; face the things you have been putting off and get them done.

- **Do something you care about**, that is meaningful for you, that pushes your buttons, that makes you feel alive. Help others, let others help you.
- **Take in everything life has to offer**, good or bad. Accept it, learn, and keep walking.

And finally, **be kind to yourself**. Do not punish yourself for what you cannot achieve or control. If you had a panic attack, do not blame yourself; take the opportunity to learn from it, to grow and know yourself better.

You are stronger than you think, and you need to find that out yourself.

ACKNOWLEDGEMENTS

Nothing in life is achieved in isolation. There are so many contributions, even if hard work and some luck travel hand-in-hand on occasion. As for most people, that is also the case for me.

I have worked hard in my life to be able to do what I like, to focus on what I am passionate about, and share my knowledge and experience with others during my clinical work, research and teaching. To be able to do so I am lucky to be able to rely on my family. They are my rock. My parents, my sister, my nieces and also now my own nuclear family: my husband, his mother, and my child. They make it all possible because they are there, present, and support me no matter what. So, thank you, Cesar, Fernanda, Ines, Tiago, Carlota, Alice, Matt, Sharon and Toby. I would be nothing without you and the experiences I have shared with you.

A special thank you to my husband Matt, who is my main support, my stability and go-to friend for the good and the bad moments, and also my editor for this work. Words would not be sufficient to say how grateful I am.

I would like to also thank my friend Heledd for always being there and my other friends and professional colleagues, who make my work feel valued and rewarding, with a special thank you to Rita Woo and Michael Worrell, whose discussions and laughs I appreciate and value immensely.

I could not write this book without my clients, without whom my career would make no sense. Thank you for sharing your lives and for walking the journey of discovery, understanding and recovery with me. My life would not be the same without all of you.

I would like to acknowledge the overwhelming contribution that the work of scientists, researchers and clinicians in the field have made to my career development and clinical practice. My gratitude goes out to the outstanding work of Jonathan S. Abramowitz, Gordon J.G. Asmundson, Martin M. Antony, David H. Barlow, Aaron T. Beck, James Bennett-Levy, Thomas D. Borkovec, David A. Clark, David M. Clark, Antonio Damásio, Graham C.L. Davey, Edna B. Foa, Dennis Greenbeger, Peter Lang, Robert L. Leahy, Joseph Ledoux, Arne Öhman, Lars-Göran Öst, Christine Purdon, Stanley J. Rachman, Ronald M. Rapee, Paul M. Salkovskis, Robert Sapolsky, Gail S. Steketee, Steven Taylor and David Veale, among others.

ENDNOTES

1. de Jonge, P., Roest, A. M., Lim, C. C. W., Florescu, S. E., Bromet, E., Stein, D., et al. (2016). Cross-national epidemiology of panic disorder and panic attacks in the world mental health surveys. *Depression and Anxiety, 33,* 1155–1177.
   de Jonge, P., Roest, A. M., Lim, C. C. W, Levinson, D., & Scott, K. M. (2018). Panic disorder and panic attacks. In K. M. Scott, P. de Jonge, D. J. Stein & R. C. Kessler (eds.), *Mental Disorders Around the World: Facts and Figures from the WHO World Mental Health Surveys.* Cambridge: Cambridge University Press.

2. American Psychiatric Association (APA). (2013). Diagnostic and statistical manual of mental disorders (5th ed.). Washington, DC: Author. pp 214.

3. de Jonge, P., Roest, A. M., Lim, C. C. W, Levinson, D., & Scott, K. M. (2018). Panic disorder and panic attacks. In K. M. Scott, P. de Jonge, D. J. Stein & R. C. Kessler (eds.), *Mental Disorders Around the World: Facts and Figures from the WHO World Mental Health Surveys.* Cambridge: Cambridge University Press.

4. de Jonge, P., Roest, A. M., Lim, C. C. W., Florescu, S. E., Bromet, E., Stein, D., et al. (2016). Cross-national epidemiology of panic disorder and panic attacks in the

world mental health surveys. *Depression and Anxiety,*
33, 1155–1177.

5. de Jonge, P., Roest, A. M., Lim, C. C. W, Levinson, D., &
Scott, K. M. (2018). Panic disorder and panic attacks. In
K. M. Scott, P. de Jonge, D. J. Stein & R. C. Kessler (eds.),
Mental Disorders Around the World: Facts and Figures
from the WHO World Mental Health Surveys. Cambridge:
Cambridge University Press.

6. Kenardy, J., Fried, L., Kraemer, H. C., & Taylor, C. B. (1992).
Psychological precursors of panic attacks. *British Journal*
of Psychiatry, 160, 668–673; Bandelow, B., Domschke, K.,
& Baldwin, D. S. (2014). *Panic disorder and Agoraphobia*
(Oxford Psychiatry Library). Oxford: Oxford University Press.

7. Barlow, D. H. (2000). Unravelling the mysteries of anxiety
and its disorders from the perspective of emotion theory.
American Psychologist, 55, 1247–1263.

USEFUL RESOURCES

General mental health resources

UK

- Heads Together: www.headstogether.org.uk
- Hub of Hope: hubofhope.co.uk
- Mental Health Foundation UK: ww.mentalhealth.org.uk
- Mind UK: www.mind.org.uk
- Rethink Mental Illness: www.rethink.org
- Samaritans: www.samaritans.org, helpline: 116 123
- Scottish Association for Mental Health (SAMH) (Scotland): www.samh.org.uk
- Shout: www.giveusashout.org, text 85258
- Young Minds: www.youngminds.org.uk

Europe

- Mental Health Europe: www.mhe-sme.org
- Mental Health Ireland: www.mentalhealthireland.ie

USA

- Help Guide: www.helpguide.org
- Mentalhealth.gov: www.mentalhealth.gov

- Mental Health America: www.mhanational.org
- National Alliance on Mental Illness (NAMI): www.nami.org
- National Institute of Mental Health: www.nimh.nih.gov
- Very Well Mind: www.verywellmind.com

Canada

- Canadian Mental Health Association: cmha.ca
- Crisis Service Canada: www.ementalhealth.ca

Australia and New Zealand

- Beyond Blue: www.beyondblue.org.au
- Head to Health: headtohealth.gov.au
- Health Direct: www.healthdirect.gov.au
- Mental Health Australia: mhaustralia.org
- Mental Health Foundation of New Zealand: www.mentalhealth.org.nz
- SANE Australia: www.sane.org

Other countries

- It's OK to Talk (India): www.itsoktotalk.in
- Pan American Mental Health Organization (North and South America): www.paho.org

Support for sufferers of panic attacks and anxiety

In the following websites you can find guidance, support, advice and treatment options available.

UK

- Anxiety UK: www.anxietyuk.org.uk, helpline: 03444 775 774
- No More Panic: www.nomorepanic.co.uk
- No panic: www.nopanic.org.uk
- Social Anxiety: www.social-anxiety.org.uk

USA

- Anxiety and Depression Association of America: www.adaa.org

Canada

- Anxiety Canada: www.anxietycanada.com

Australia and New Zealand

- Anxiety New Zealand Trust: www.anxiety.org.nz
- Black Dog Institute: www.blackdoginstitute.org.au

Support for suicidal thoughts

If you are finding it difficult to cope or know someone who is, and need to be heard without judgment or pressure, you can find information and support from the following:

- Crisis Text Line (USA, Canada, Ireland, UK): www.crisistextline.org

UK

- Campaign Against Living Miserably (CALM): www.thecalmzone.net
- PAPYRUS (dedicated to the prevention of young suicide): www.papyrus-uk.org
- The Samaritans: www.samaritans.org

USA

- American Foundation for Suicide Prevention: afsp.org
- National Suicide Prevention Lifeline: suicidepreventionlifeline.org

Canada

- Canada Suicide Prevention Crisis Service: www.crisisservicescanada.ca

Australia and New Zealand

- Lifeline Australia: www.lifeline.org.au

BIBLIOGRAPHY

American Psychiatric Association (APA). (2000). Diagnostic and statistical manual of mental disorders (4th ed., text rev.). Washington, DC: Author.

American Psychiatric Association (APA). (2013). Diagnostic and statistical manual of mental disorders (5th ed.). Washington, DC: Author.

Bandelow, B., Domschke, K., & Baldwin, D. S. (2014). *Panic disorder and Agoraphobia (Oxford Psychiatry Library)*. Oxford: Oxford University Press.

Barlow, D. H. (2000). Unravelling the mysteries of anxiety and its disorders from the perspective of emotion theory. *American Psychologist, 55,* 1247–1263.

Barlow, D. H. (2002). *Anxiety and its disorders: The nature and treatment of anxiety and panic*. New York: The Guilford Press.

Beck, A. T., Emery, G., & Greenberg, R. L. (1985). *Anxiety disorders and phobias: a cognitive perspective*. New York: Basic Books.

Borkovec, T. D. (1994). The nature, functions, and origins of worry. In G. C. L. Davey & F. Tallis (eds.). *Worrying: Perspectives on theory, assessment, and treatment*. New York: Wiley.

Borkovec, T. D. (1994). The nature, functions, and origins of worry. In G. C. L. Daey & F. Tallis (eds.). *Worrying:*

Perspectives on theory, assessment, and treatment. New York: Wiley.

Borkovec, T. D., Day, W. J., & Stober, J. (1998). Worry: A cognitive phenomenon intimately linked to affective, physiological and interpersonal behaviour processes. *Cognitive Therapy and Research, 22*, 561–576.

Boswell, J. F., Thompson-Hollands, J., Farchione, T. J., & Barlow, B. H. (2013). Intolerance of uncertainty: A common factor in the treatment of emotional disorders. *Journal of Clinical Psychology, 69*, 630–645.

Brown, T. A., & Cash, T. F. (1990). The phenomenon of non-clinical panic: parameters of panic, fear, and avoidance. *Journal of Anxiety Disorders, 4*, 15–29.

Clark, D. M. (1996). Panic disorder: from theory to therapy. In P. M. Salkovskis (ed.). *Frontiers of cognitive therapy* (pp. 318–344). New York: Guilford.

Clark, D. M. (1999). Anxiety Disorders: Why they persist and how to treat them. *Behaviour Research and Therapy, 37*, 5–27.

Clark, A. D., & Beck, A. T. (2010). *Cognitive Therapy of Anxiety Disorders: Science and Practice*. New York: The Guilford Press.

Clark, D. M., & Salkovskis, P. M. (in press). Panic Disorder. In K. Hawton, P. M. Salkovskis, J. Kirk, & D. M. Clark. (eds). *Cognitive Behaviour Therapy: A Practical Guide (2nd ed.)*. Oxford: Oxford University Press.

Craske, M. G., Miller, P. P., Rotunda, R., & Barlow, D. H. (1990). A descriptive report of features of initial unexpected panic attacks in minimal and extensive avoiders. *Behaviour Research and Therapy, 28*, 395–400.

Davey, C. L. (1997). *Phobias: A Handbook of Theory, Research and Treatment*. Chichester: Wiley and Sons.

Foa, E. B., & Kozak, M. J. (1986). Emotional processing of fear: Exposure to corrective information. *Psychological Bulletin, 99,* 20–35.

de Jonge, P., Roest, A. M., Lim, C. C. W., Florescu, S. E., Bromet, E., Stein, D., et al. (2016). Cross-national epidemiology of panic disorder and panic attacks in the world mental health surveys. *Depression and Anxiety, 33,* 1155–1177.

de Jonge, P., Roest, A. M., Lim, C. C. W, Levinson, D., & Scott, K. M. (2018). Panic disorder and panic attacks. In K. M. Scott, P. de Jonge, D. J. Stein & R. C. Kessler (eds.). *Mental Disorders Around the World: Facts and Figures from the WHO World Mental Health Surveys*. Cambridge: Cambridge University Press.

Kenardy, J., Fried, L., Kraemer, H. C., & Taylor, C. B. (1992). Psychological precursors of panic attacks. *British Journal of Psychiatry, 160,* 668–673.

Kessler, R. C., Chiu, W. T., Demler, O., & Walters, E. E. (2005). Lifetime prevalence and age-of-onset distributions of the DSM-IV disorders in the National Comorbidity Survey Replication. *Archives of General Psychiatry, 62,* 593–602.

Kushner, M.G., Krueger, R., Frye, B., Peterson, J. (2008). Epidemiological perspectives on co-occurring anxiety disorder and substance use disorder. In S. H. Stewart, P. J. Conrod (eds.). *Anxiety and Substance Use Disorders: The Vicious Cycle of Comorbidity*. New York: Springer.

Lang, P. J., Davis, M., Ohman, A. (2000). Fear and Anxiety: Animal models and human cognitive psychophysiology. *Journal of Affective Disorders, 61,* 137–159.

LeDoux, J. (1996). *The Emotional Brain: The Mysterious Underpinnings of Emotional Life*. New York: Oxford University Press.

LeDoux, J. (2015). *Anxious: The Modern Mind in the Age of Anxiety*. England: Oneworld Publications.

LeDoux J. (1998). Fear and the brain: Where have we been, and where are we going? *Biological Psychiatry, 44*, 1229–1238.

LoBue, V., & DeLoache, J. S. (2008). Detecting the snake in the grass. Attention to fear-relevant stimuli by adults and young children. *Psychological Science, 19*, 284–289.

Öhman, A. (1993). Fear and anxiety as emotional phenomena: Clinical phenomenology, evolutionary perspectives, and information processing mechanisms. In M. Lewis, & J. M. Haviland (eds.). *Handbook of Emotions*. New York: Guilford.

Öhman, A. (2009). Of snakes and faces: An evolutionary perspective on the psychology of fear. *Scandinavian Journal of Psychology, 50*, 543–552.

Öhman, A., & Mineka, S. (2001). Fears, phobias, and preparedness: Toward an evolved module of fear and fear learning. *Psychological Review, 108*, 483–522.

Öhman, A., & Soares, J. J. F. (1994). Unconscious anxiety: Phobic responses to masked stimuli. *Journal of Abnormal Psychology, 103*, 231–240.

Olsson, A., & Phelps, E. A. (2007). Social learning of fear. *Nature Neuroscience, 10*, 1095–1102.

Porto, P. R., Oliveira, L., Mari, J., Volchan, E., Figueira, I., & Ventura, P. (2009). Does cognitive behavioral therapy change the brain? A systematic review of neuroimaging in anxiety disorders. *Journal of Neuropsychiatry and Clinical Neurosciences, 21*, 114–125.

Salkovskis, P. M. (1991). The importance of behaviour in the maintenance of panic and anxiety. *Behavioural Psychotherapy, 19*, 6–19.

Sapolky, R. (2017). *Behave: The Biology of Humans at Our Best and Worst*. London: Penguin Random House.

Seligman, M. E. P. (1971). Phobias and preparedness. *Behaviour Therapy, 2*, 307–320.

Wolpe, J. (1969). *The Practice of Behavior Therapy*. New York: Pergamon Press.

Wolpe, J., & Lazarus, A. A. (1966). *Behavior therapy Techniques: A Guide to the Treatment of Neuroses*. New York: Pergamon Press.

ABOUT US

Welbeck Balance publishes books dedicated to changing lives. Our mission is to deliver life-enhancing books to help improve your wellbeing so that you can live your life with greater clarity and meaning, wherever you are on life's journey. Our Trigger books are specifically devoted to opening up conversations about mental health and wellbeing.

Welbeck Balance and Trigger are part of the Welbeck Publishing Group – a globally recognized independent publisher based in London. Welbeck are renowned for our innovative ideas, production values and developing long-lasting content. Our books have been translated into over 30 languages in more than 60 countries around the world.

If you love books, then join the club and sign up to our newsletter for exclusive offers, extracts, author interviews and more information.

To find out more and to sign up, visit: www.welbeckpublishing.com
Twitter.com/welbeckpublish
Instagram.com/welbeckpublish
Facebook.com/welbeckuk

Find out more about Trigger: www.triggerhub.org
Twitter.com@Triggercalm
Facebook.com @Triggercalm
Instagram.com @Triggercalm

WELBECK
BALANCE